ALSO BY WENDY MOGEL, PH.D.

The Blessing of a Skinned Knee:
Using Jewish Teachings to Raise Self-Reliant Children

THE BLESSING OF A B MINUS

USING JEWISH TEACHINGS TO RAISE RESILIENT TEENAGERS

Wendy Mogel, Ph.D.

SCRIBNER

New York   London   Toronto   Sydney

SCRIBNER
A Division of Simon & Schuster, Inc.
1230 Avenue of the Americas
New York, NY 10020

First Scribner hardcover edition October 2010

SCRIBNER and design are registered trademarks of The Gale Group, Inc.,
used under license by Simon & Schuster, Inc., the publisher of this work.

For information about special discounts for bulk purchases,
please contact Simon & Schuster Special Sales at
1-866-506-1949 or business@simonandschuster.com.

The Simon & Schuster Speakers Bureau can bring authors
to your live event. For more information or to book an event
contact the Simon & Schuster Speakers Bureau at
1-866-248-3049 or visit our website at www.simonspeakers.com.

DESIGNED BY ERICH HOBBING

Manufactured in the United States of America

4 6 8 10 9 7 5

Library of Congress Control Number: 2010017762

ISBN 978-1-4165-4203-2
ISBN 978-1-4391-8749-4 (ebook)

The story of Honi the Circle Maker from *The Hungry Clothes and Other Jewish Folktales*
© by Peninnah Schram. Used with permission from Sterling Publishing Company, Inc.
"Head, Heart" from *The Collected Stories of Lydia Davis*, by Lydia Davis. Copyright © 2009 by Lydia Davis.
Reprinted by permission of Farrar, Straus, and Giroux, LLC.

TO SUSANNA AND EMMA

Contents

"Mother, may I go out to swim?"
"Yes, my darling daughter.
Hang your clothes on a hickory limb
But don't go near the water."
—Mother Goose

Baruch b'al milchamot.
Blessed is the one who engages in battles.

Author's Note

Unless otherwise noted, all Jewish teachings in the text of this book are drawn from the following sources: Biblical commentary and most translations from the Hebrew are from Rabbi W. Gunther Plaut's *The Torah: A Modern Commentary* (New York: Union of American Hebrew Congregations, 1981) and Rabbi Abraham Ben Isiah and Rabbi Benjamin Sharfman's *The Pentateuch and Rashi's Commentary* (New York: S. S. and R. Publishing, 1949). Other translations are from the Jewish Publication Society's *Tanakh: A New Translation of the Holy Scriptures* (Philadelphia and Jerusalem: 1985). When choosing among the three, I often created a composite.

Quotes from Moses Maimonides are from Philip Birnbaum's translation and annotation of the *Mishneh Torah: Maimonides Code of Law and Ethics* (New York: Hebrew Publishing Company, 1944). Teachings from the Babylonian Talmud are from the Schottenstein Edition of the *Talmud Bavli* (Artscroll Series, New York: Mesorah Publications, 1993). The quotations about Rabbi Girondi's view of repentance in chapter 8 and Rabbi Judah the Prince's view of pleasure in chapter 9 were previously used by Rabbi Joseph Telushkin in his classic compendium *Jewish Wisdom* (New York: William Morrow, 1994).

THE BLESSING OF A B MINUS

The Hidden Blessings of Raising Teenagers

After the publication of *The Blessing of a Skinned Knee*, people often asked me why I'd written the book. My answer was that I wrote the book to remind myself to do what it said. And mostly, it worked. Using the Jewish teachings I'd written about, I was able to resist the extremes of overprotection, overscheduling, overindulgence, and the sky-high expectations that were the norm in the Los Angeles neighborhood in which I was raising my two young daughters. I was clear and strategic about teaching my children to honor mother and father; I also worked to honor *them* by respecting both their talents and limitations. I reminded myself daily of the Talmudic dictum that says every parent is obligated to teach their child how to swim—a philosophy I applied by letting my daughters climb really tall trees, use sharp knives, cook with a hot pan, and, of course, because I live in Southern California, learn to swim and jump and dive in the deep end while they were still very young.

When my first book was published, my girls were nine and thirteen years old, and I gazed confidently ahead to their adolescence. When it comes to teenagers, I am a professional. Literally. I am a social-clinical psychologist, which means I am trained to look at emotional problems in their cultural context. My specialty is parenting and normal child development. I've been working with families for thirty years. I know the theories of individuation, the effect of puberty on mood, the way circadian rhythms disrupt teens' sleep cycles, and the teenaged thirst for dopamine (the neurochemical of risk and excitement). I am well aware of the negative impact of our speedy, wired, competitive, and coarse culture on the development of good character in young people. I am alert to modern teens' vulnerability to anxiety, eating disorders, self-injury, depression, learning and attention problems, and substance abuse.

I imagined that with my professional and religious bag of tricks in hand, I'd guide my daughters safely past all the usual hazards of adolescence. As they left their tween years, my daughters would become more responsible, more mature, and better family citizens. Under my thoughtful guidance, we'd develop common interests; we'd enjoy deeper conversations. The wheels of daily family life would glide more smoothly now that we had these tall, intelligent, articulate, inventive helpmates on the team.

This is not what happened.

Instead, as my girls grew older, the pleasant choreography of daily life evaporated. In its place arrived unrelenting power struggles over every conceivable topic: waking up (they couldn't); going to bed (they wouldn't); chores ("Mom! I can't! I have band practice after school and a big test tomorrow"). The lovely neatness of their rooms was gone, a casualty of teen blindness to clothes and drinking glasses on the floor. Their pretty outfits were rejected for what looked like ragged cast-offs. Their contribution to conversations mostly consisted of monosyllabic sentences through closed doors or pointed insults hurled at my husband and me. At times there were so many troubles and resentments brewing in our house that I questioned my fitness as a mother; I wondered if it was too late. Had I already ruined my children? I reminded myself to pick battles. *But which ones?* I wondered. There were so many battles to choose from! I told myself to let them make their own mistakes, the teen version of allowing them to skin their knees. But now this advice seemed naive. *What if they get into really big trouble, the kind that wreaks permanent havoc on their grades, their health, their futures?* In my practice I had helped hundreds of families, but I felt helpless with mine.

In addition to my anger and confusion, I also felt grief. To raise young children is to drink daily at the font of tenderness and physical affection: "Mommy and Daddy, please lie down with me . . . read me one more book . . . stay with me till I fall asleep!" Now signs appeared on my daughters' doors: "Keep out. This means you." Me. The one who had changed their vomit-covered sheets and sang just the right lullaby and gently rocked and rocked and rocked them. *Keep out. This means you.*

Then I brightened. I remembered that I had Judaism! When my children were younger, Judaism had helped me recast everyday parenting problems into questions of everyday holiness. It reminded me that our children are a loan from God and we are simply stewards. It guided me toward the basic but powerful principles of moderation, celebration, and sanctification. Yes, I'd redouble my efforts to bring Jewish rituals into our home. I would go back to baking challah from scratch. I'd bake it that very Friday night. I imagined the smell wafting up to the girls' rooms and, just as the sacrifices at the ancient holy temple "were pleasing to the Lord," they would also be delighted, following the scent downstairs. They'd stop at the landing and smile at the beautifully set Shabbat table, eager to engage in a ritual that had so reliably provided us with family togetherness and spiritual elevation for so many years. We would discuss the Torah portion about *shalom bayit* (peace in the home), and, chagrined but hopeful, the girls would ask how they might make amends for their crappy attitudes, lack of gratitude, and laziness.

This did not happen, either.

That Friday night, after the girls explained that they were too busy to have Shabbat dinner with us, I found myself alone with my husband, my loaf of challah, the grape juice and the wine, and ample time for reflection. I decided that going back to Judaism still had potential, but that it might be best to deemphasize the family rituals and instead focus on shoring up my own spiritual stance.

Once again, I discovered practical wisdom in ancient rabbinic teachings. I reread one of the foundational stories of Judaism, the journey from Egypt to the Promised Land. I had often heard this trip described as the adolescence of the Jewish people, the time between their "childhood" in slavery and their maturity as governors of the Promised Land, but now I saw the analogy with the eyes of someone who is actually on the trip. Moses had to put up with forty years of directing a flock of whiners and complainers. Whenever he turned his back, even for a minute, they made the kind of trouble that is familiar to parents of teenagers: overstuffing themselves on manna; worshipping a glittering false idol; throwing a bacchanal. When he tried to reason with the people, they were sarcastic: "Was it for want of graves in Egypt that you brought us to this awful, awful place?" they asked. They threatened to revolt. They moaned and cried that they wished they could be slaves again. The biblical commentaries explain that although there was a relatively quick, direct path through the desert, God intentionally led Moses on a roundabout route for decades. The adolescence of the Jewish people had to be long and difficult enough for it to really take, for them to develop hard-won wisdom and, at last, grow up. No shortcuts allowed.

That lesson for parents—no shortcuts allowed—is something I'd lost sight of. My expertise as a psychologist couldn't protect my family from the vicissitudes of adolescence, and no wonder: Raising teenagers has always been hard. It *has* to be hard. Judaism teaches us that the agonizing transition of adolescence is all part of what is called *tzar giddul banim*, the necessary pain of raising children. I knew from my professional life that most of this pain is caused by the important work teenagers do when they begin to separate from their parents. They move away and establish their own identity, yet at the same time they long for security and comfort. They kick at authority, unconsciously trying to make parents less attractive so it will be easier to leave them. They cling to their friends, who are as awkward and unsteady as they are. It is their job to oppose their parents, to make mistakes in order to acquire a deeply felt sense of right and wrong, to reject Mom and Dad in order to fully realize their own sense of self. This "necessary pain" must be experienced. If parents do not treat this journey with respect and dignity, if we insist (as I did) on trying to find a shortcut, if we do not allow teenagers the time they need to kvetch and make stupid mistakes and reject us, they won't get where they need to go. Again, I began writing a book because I had to, because I needed to remind myself to love my teenagers' rough, uneven path across the desert.

I found myself drawn back to the advice given in traditional Judaism to say blessings, or prayers of gratitude, at least one hundred times a day. There are prescribed prayers to say upon rising in the morning, after using the bathroom, before eating the first ripe fruit of a season, before putting on new clothes. There is even a prayer to say when bad things happen: "Thank you, God, for this test of my spiritual elevation." I realized it could be a wise spiritual practice for all of us parents to say a blessing over the necessary pain of adolescent separation, too. Not because we should adopt a falsely bright, "Everything's peachy at our house!" attitude, but because the pain is a sign that adolescence is proceeding normally. It is crucial to acquire an understanding of this feature of adolescent development, because without it we take our teens' normal rebellion personally. We get enmeshed in our teens' problems. We take a snapshot of our teens in their current phase and mistake it for the epic movie of their entire life. We become so entangled with our children that we are unable to step back, think calmly, and provide clear-headed leadership. Instead of guiding our teens toward Jewish values like self-reliance, self-control, moderation, and sanctified celebration, we make our daily choices based on media-generated fears or on our perception of what looks good on college applications.

My suggestion that bewildered parents view adolescence as a blessing is more than a sweet-sounding philosophy. At an age when your kids don't tolerate religion, you can respectfully take the baton for a while. This means you cultivate an attitude of gratitude, shifting your own perspective rather than trying to control your child. Each of the chapters to come describes a common complaint about teenagers and reconceives it as a sign of good health, psychological development, or spiritual progression:

- Bizarre teen behavior, so annoyingly not in line with your dreams and plans, is a sign that your teen's unique personality is unfolding. When you, the parent, practice charitable acceptance of your teen's self-expression, you increase the chances that she will blossom mentally, morally, and spiritually.
- Teenaged rudeness is a paradox. It lets you know that your teen is trying desperately to separate from you *and* that you are the "safe" person who can receive their frustration with not yet being all grown up. This is your chance to set reasonable limits for your teen and to demonstrate that mature adults are not easily provoked by bad manners.
- One of the ways teens learn about the importance of hard work is by suffering the consequences of their procrastination and laziness. A wise parent will resist interfering with those natural consequences, even if it means allowing a child to take a lower-than-wished-for grade.
- Materialism and self-centeredness are normal during this period of rapid and shifting identity formation. Just as a pregnant woman focuses inward, thinking about how her body is changing and fantasizing about what her baby will look like, adolescents are preoccupied as they give birth to themselves. Parents can practice tolerance of this phase while spotting opportunities to teach teens how to think about the future and beyond their egocentric concerns.

- When teens break the rules, or even the law, it is often because they aren't satisfied with a merely rote knowledge of our ethical system. What's right? What's wrong? Do adults mean what they say when they make rules? Are there exceptions? By requiring teens to make amends for their wrongs *and* by helping them channel some of their wild spirit, parents allow their teens to acquire an in-depth knowledge of our moral code.
- Teens get into hot water all the time. They court drama and are poor predictors of disaster. This provides an excellent opportunity for learning self-reliance: how to solve problems and how to mine difficult circumstances for their benefits.
- Staying up late is sometimes a teen's shot at independence, and goofing around is a way to ease the stresses of growing up. Parents should respect a teen's need to wind down and protect their need for rest and fun.
- Finally, limited experimentation with alcohol, physical intimacy, and even drugs teaches teens how to regulate these powerful experiences and keep themselves safe while they are still under your guidance.

I know it's not easy to convert your teens' struggles into blessings. It requires both insight and courage. The Hebrew word for Egypt is *mitzrayim*. It means a narrow place. The Jews escaped from Egypt and were *b'midbar,* in the desert, the wilderness, traveling with no guarantee of what would be on the other side. The new and better land was only a promise. They had to have faith in their leader, Moses, and in an unknowable future. Adolescence, too, is a time of change with no blueprint or guarantees. It's tempting to think that we should protect teens during the desert crossing of adolescence. But that's not our job. Our job is to guide them through it.

This is another blessing of raising adolescents: It's the best opportunity you will ever have to develop your leadership qualities. When your children were young, it was appropriate for you to guide them actively. You allowed them to skin their knees and learn from their mistakes, but you also performed many hands-on functions like checking their backpacks for stray homework assignments, making sure their hair was brushed, and seeing that they wore hats and gloves in cold weather. Now, as the parent of a teenager, your job is counterintuitive. Just as a corporate executive has to resist micromanagement to be effective, it's time for you to practice detachment, to do less instead of more.

Detachment, practiced properly, is neither cold nor unloving. It doesn't mean that you walk away from your parenting duties. Quite the opposite. Detachment is a balancing act that requires both *rachmanut* (compassion) and *tsimtsum* ("contraction of divine energy"). This is an effective spiritual model for relinquishing control over children based on God's relationship with us, his children. According to the Jewish mystics, originally everything was God; God's light and energy filled up the entire universe. But in order to make room for the world to expand, to fill it with plants and animals and people, God had to inhale, to pull back and contract his power. Parents of teens can do the same. As leaders of our children, it's essential for us to step back from the urgency, the mistakes, the heartbreaks, the rejection. We practice *rachmanut* and *tsimtsum* by watching the dramas of the day as committed but slightly amused observers. The school-wide epidemic of mononucleosis; the moving violation your son incurs when he's caught doing "doughnuts" in an icy parking lot; your daughter's grief and outrage when she is dumped by her best friend—respond with concern *and* detachment. Know the difference between a crisis and an emergency. Don't worry too much about being popular; don't act too quickly; do develop hobbies or interests outside of your family life to absorb some of the leftover tension; and in general, try to find the humor in a large part of what transpires. By taking a deep breath and withdrawing, you make space for your child to grow.

A Jewish approach to blessings takes us away from a myopic view of the day-to-day. ("My daughter got a B minus on a math test! The end is near.") It carries us both down and up. We go *down* to a deeper level of our own faith, because we are sorely tested. Just as our children become their most difficult, and at the time when everyone else around us has swallowed the Kool-Aid of fear and anxiety, we are asked to take the long, long view of adolescent development. And we go *up* to a greater experience and wisdom. During the ten years between the publication of *Skinned Knee* and the book you are now reading, I've seen the children of kind, thoughtful, sensible parents (these parents include myself, my clients, my friends, my family, the parents at my lectures) wrestle with troubles, and then I've seen almost every one of them grow into an admirable and interesting young adult. Now that my daughters are grown, I remember how distressed, confused, and frightened I was by their adolescence, but I also look back with buckets of delight at the traveling circus of their teen years, at their amazing friendships and adventures, at their concerted efforts to figure out how to grow up. As parents of teenagers, we are asked to lead from a new position of calm authority, not just for ourselves and our children but for community, for the work of *tikkun olam,* healing the cosmic tear in the universe.

CHAPTER 2

The Blessing of Strange Fruit:

Accepting the Unique Glory of Your Teen

A high school dean told me about a student who kept her involvement in drama club secret from her mother and father. The girl's parents were devoted to getting her into a top college and considered this activity frivolous and not transcript-worthy. So when the teen attended rehearsals, she told her parents that she was studying at the library or a friend's house. Everyone—friends, drama teacher, and other cast members—helped her keep the secret. Her parents never found out, never attended one of her performances, and therefore never saw their daughter doing the thing she loved most.

When I told this story to the director of a drama department at a different high school, he said that when parents worry about how "just being in plays" will look on the transcript, he explains that:

Each.

Play.

Goes.

On.

A.

Separate.

Line.

"See, it's transcript real estate!" he tells the parents. "Drama club provides plenty of land in the right district!" And they are relieved.

When I tell this story in lectures, audience members laugh in mingled horror and relief. Horror that any parent would miss their child's star turn; relief that they're not the only ones who, amid the strenuous work of guiding their teens successfully into adulthood, sometimes fail to recognize or respect their children's true talents and dreams.

In *The Blessing of a Skinned Knee,* I talked about accepting children as they are—not tiny champions who are exceptional at everything, but gloriously ordinary children, made in God's image. It is not much of a stretch for most parents to see God's presence in their silken, laughing six-year-olds, especially with their future spreading so safely off in the far, far distance.

But at the first whiff of middle school, even the most laid-back parents find it difficult to practice loving acceptance of their children. When children hit their tweens, it suddenly seems that there is so much more at stake for them than there was for us when we were growing up, so much more danger on the horizon. Conversations with other parents turn on the importance of securing the right niche for their child before she enters the wilderness of high school: *Knowing that Rachel doesn't have a lot of natural self-discipline, I'm afraid that if she doesn't get into the gifted and talented program, she could end up hanging out with the potheads.* At parties, parents no longer talk about where to buy healthy snacks; now the preferred topic is the cutthroat process of college applications: *Did you read on CollegeConfidential.com that kids who play wind instruments increase their chances of getting a scholarship? That's why Jeremy is studying oboe. And have you had any luck finding a new math tutor for Benjamin?* And as early as sixth grade, choosing electives becomes a fraught decision: *Can Alison afford to take a World Languages class, or is it time to start developing a specialty in French?*

We decide that it was fine to revel in our child's ordinary glory when she was younger, but no longer. Now "it counts." Ordinary is no longer good enough—not when our child is out in public like a walking billboard of our family's priorities, not if these are the years that permanently shape his character, not if she is going to make it into college. There is a strong temptation to treat adolescents as if they are products to be developed and packaged for inspection. Outstanding sports performance? Check. Proficient in at least one musical instrument? Check. Upper-tier SATs? Check. Slender and fit? Check. Student leader? Check. Pushing for anything less than all-around perfection feels like dereliction of parental duty. One mother confided in me that she worried about her middle son:

He's such a good guy. He still loves model trains and playing with his little sister. Everybody likes having him around, but he hasn't made a mark or found a true passion yet. He's only fourteen, but when I look at the attitude of the other parents, it feels like there are only two positions: ahead and behind. That makes me think I should "do something" about Adam, push him harder, make him put aside his trains for something less juvenile. It breaks my heart because he's the happiest person in the family. And that's a good quality, isn't it?

It is not loving to expect a child to be good at everything all the time—to be a smooth and sleek academic, social, artistic, and athletic machine. It is not realistic to expect perfection of *anyone*. When we do, our teens suffer. I belong to a group of school counselors, and over the past ten years the tales of the hidden toll, the dark side of teens' striving for perfection, have become the most common topic of discussion at our meetings. The counselors describe boys who relieve the pressure by hiding out in Dune or Halo or World of Warcraft. Or they go on homework strikes. These boys have more homework than their parents ever did, but they are unable to articulate how boring and oppressive they find their work. Without the maturity to locate a middle ground between perfection and defeat, they choose surrender. What do girls do? They take the pain out on themselves. Poet Adrienne Rich writes that when girls can't touch or name their anger, they "drive it inward like a rusted nail." They try to look perfect on the outside, but in private they starve, scratch, cut, or burn themselves. The pain they feel physically relieves the pressure they feel inside. One girl I saw in my therapy practice said simply: *I injure myself when I feel I have failed at something.*

Our culture has such a narrow definition of success: grades, gregariousness, ambition, and appearance. While each of these qualities can fit onto a longer, deeper, and more nuanced list of ingredients for a satisfying adult life, we forget that our children come to us *b'ztelim Elohim*, made in God's image. This is no less true in adolescence than when they are preschoolers. They are magnificent in their own way, not necessarily in the way we'd like them to be. Some teens have talents and traits that are easy to overlook or difficult to measure with a number: They can bond with animals or instantly find common ground with the person sitting next to them on the bus or have a wild but harmonious sense of color. And some are just different, and that doesn't by definition mean defective.

Teens are also works in progress; they are naturally uneven and unsure. The qualities you see today may be gone by Monday. God and nature give them their developmental pace, and we parents cannot speed it up or slow it down. Accepting your teen's individuality and natural evolution is one of the most difficult challenges you'll face as a parent. It means working with, instead of against, your child's unique developmental timetable, endowment, temperament, and style. But your bedrock acceptance of your teen's God-given spirit is also wildly important for the flowering of your child's gifts, for her confidence and zest for life, for her self-respect and respect for you.

It will be difficult to offer your unstinting acceptance of your teen unless you recognize the forces behind the frenzied drive for perfection. There are many factors at work, but three of the most important are parents' own unfulfilled dreams; fears about college and the future; and the pain of their teenager's rejection.

BIG DREAMS, BUT WHOSE?

It is natural for parents to nurture both public and secret dreams for their children's future. Yet these dreams should be based on the child's actual desires and abilities, not the ones we might wish them to have. So many sensible, intelligent, devoted parents imagine a future for their child that goes something like this:

Our son gets straight A's and is captain of the lacrosse team. He's designed a Web program to help teachers create their own computerized multiple-choice tests and it's been such a success that the profits will cover the small gap between his tuition and the giant scholarship offered to him by his college of choice, and, oh, he and his girlfriend give surf lessons to underprivileged children in the summer.

But there are other dreams, too. One mother of two sons told me, "I just hoped that one of them would be gay, and he'd become a set designer for art films and travel the world on cruises and he'd entertain me and my friends with witty stories when we're in the nursing home." Or maybe you always loved art but ended up practicing law and here's your daughter with *so much* aptitude for painting.

Parents should want to be proud of their children, but be careful. We cross an important line when we demand a predetermined or unrealistic set of accomplishments for our teens. Your son as scholar-athlete-entrepreneur-humanitarian? Few, if any, adults possess all of these talents. Is it fair to expect your son to? It's also dangerous to expect children to carry out your own unfulfilled dreams: of living the artistic life, of effortlessly compatible romantic relationships, of impressive professional careers.

Parents who can't accept themselves—their own lives or looks or achievements—are especially at risk for wanting their children to be everything they're not. I frequently talk to parents who are angry at their teens for not being better students, athletes, competitors, or leaders. When their children disappoint them, the parents take it very, very personally:

You were supposed to play the cello, or at least the guitar.

You were supposed to love reading.

You weren't supposed to struggle with weight (like I have all my life) and especially not lose the struggle so publicly.

You weren't supposed to get in trouble at the school where I am a board member.

You weren't supposed to be so socially awkward when you have had such supportive, emotionally literate parents.

Parents who transfer their disappointments onto their teenagers are falling into what is probably an age-old trap. It's always been easy for parents to see teens as their last shot at realizing all their old, unlived dreams. But I think it's more common now because teens have few other obvious functions in the family. It was once standard practice for a community to harness the natural energy and bravado of teenagers, putting them to work as farmhands or domestic help or tribal guardsmen. Today most of our teens are protected from anything that looks like rough or dangerous labor. We put them to work in a different way: studying until midnight and spending all weekend at travel hockey tournaments. Their job? To bring glory and reassurance to the family. Parents rarely acknowledge these goals for their teens out loud, but if they did, they would sound something like this:

If Marnie boosts her SATs by just a hundred points, we'll have it made. Together with the rest of her profile this will make her the star of the class. Score one for stay-at-home moms!

Now that Tyler is playing varsity soccer and is captain of the swim team, my father might finally appreciate that what I've done with my life measures up. Compared to his other grandchildren, there's no contest.

But living out their parents' (or parents' parents') dreams is a terrible burden for teenagers to shoulder, one as oppressive as long, hard days tilling the fields.

Some parents don't understand how clearly their disappointment is transmitted to their teenagers or how deeply it affects them. The administrator of a girls' school asked her students, "What do you want your parents to know? What do you want me to say to them at back-to-school night?" The girls replied:

"Tell them I'm trying as hard as I can and I'm not as smart as they think I am."

"I can't be good at everything."

"Don't panic if I eat one Cheeto or get one B."

One elite high school conducted a survey that included a question asking the students to name their greatest fear. The school counselor told me she expected the students to say they worried about someone in their family getting sick, or getting bad grades, or losing their friends, or terrorism, or not getting into college, but the answer they gave more often than any other single answer was "My greatest fear is disappointing my parents."

It is not your child's job to live your dreams. When we demand that our children carry out the family's ambitions, we are not just creating unhappy, pressured, self-defeating young adults. We are snubbing God's wishes for our children. A cornerstone of Jewish thought is that God created each of us to fulfill a specific purpose during life in this world. Each person is responsible for discovering and carrying out their divinely intended purpose. As parents, we cannot determine what our children's path toward holy service will look like. Nor can we determine the destination. But by encouraging them to understand their unique strengths, we help them take the first steps.

BUT . . . BUT . . . IT'S COLLEGE!

Our culture tells us that we face quickly diminishing resources of every kind—good enough colleges, jobs, ozone . . . a scarcity of future itself— and that only the hyperaccomplished will survive. At the same time, technological progress has become the controlling metaphor for our lives; like the Web, everything we do seems transparent and permanent.

One false move on the part of even a very young teen, and the child has mortgaged his future, will never get into college, never get a job, never recover. It's harder than ever for parents to accept their teenagers because it feels as if there's no more room for the trial and error of adolescence, for childishness or clumsiness or bad attitudes. The steady thrum of anxiety causes parents to focus on the appearance of success and stability: grades, popularity, sports skills, and looks. And the kids feel this stringency, this scarcity economy, too. One fifteen-year-old girl said to me, "I feel like every minute of every day my whole future is on the line."

Nowhere does parents' anxiety about their teen's futures come into sharper relief than in that grand acceptance derby: college admissions. For many parents, the fierce competition for places at the top colleges is evidence that *all* the good things in life are scarce and growing scarcer. They believe that if their kids aren't accepted at the right college, they'll also miss out on meaningful work, quality health insurance, and the ability to provide for themselves and their families. College counselors have observed the way this fear interferes with good judgment in even the most thoughtful parents. Many believe that the ebb and flow of a child's natural evolution do not make for good reading on a college transcript. They can barely tolerate slowing down, much less ebbing. Like the parents who disapproved of their daughter joining drama club, these parents commandeer their teen's academic and personal life with an unblinking view toward impressing college admissions boards:

I have to do it for him or it won't get done.

He has to take a pre-AP course now, in eighth grade, or he won't be set up to take APs later on. And without APs on his transcript, he's looking at a state school, maybe not even the main campus of a state school.

No, he can't take time off from Model United Nations to join film club. Everyone knows film club is code for "slacker kid."

We need to hire a professional to polish his personal statement because everyone else does. It's not a level playing field from the start.

Teenagers who are running the transcript gauntlet plan their overstuffed schedules with military precision. They come home later than their parents, work longer hours, and go to bed later. When parents act as if their child's future—and parental love—is riding on every test grade, the teens turn into prematurely anguished, disconnected thirty-five-year-olds.

Sending your children out into an economically uncertain world, one that is continually remaking itself, is terrifying. But this has always been true. *Bitachon*—trust in God—does not come naturally, and this is why the rabbis have always made such a point of emphasizing its importance. It is the familiar "let go and let God" formula. Our fears about an apocalyptic future say less about reality than about our lack of trust in reality. Here's the paradox: Parents need to place more emphasis on a loving acceptance of the dizzying spiral of adolescent development than on a narrow, focused effort to make their teenagers college-worthy. By doing this, parents provide the spiritual nourishment their children need to fulfill their potential, to reach the promised land of adulthood with their vitality intact.

YOU REJECT ME? I'LL REJECT YOU!

In the previous chapter I described *tzar giddul banim,* the pain of raising children. It's supposed to be hard. But most parents are surprised at how painful it is when their teenagers—formerly cuddly, adoring toddlers— begin the difficult work of separation.

To make this process of moving away and establishing their own identity more bearable, teenagers need to make you less attractive so that it will eventually be easier to leave you.

Just when it seems that their entire future is riding on their good sense and good behavior, they become rude, disrespectful, and ungrateful. Like the frustrating clients psychotherapists call "help-rejecting complainers," teenagers ignore your advice. Through their words or their silence, they insult your choices, your point of view, your essence. They deftly attack whatever you hold most dear or feel most insecure about: *How can you stand living in a house decorated like this? You call this dinner? You call those friends? You call that a fun day?* They demean the pathetic contents of the refrigerator, the length of your jeans, or what they consider your eccentric pronunciations of common words. *No one says "WH-en" or "WH-ite." They just say "wen" and "wite" like a normal person. WH-en are you going to realize that?* They turn away from you, from the cozy family cocoon you've spent so much money and energy to create, and form their own protective tribe. They develop convictions, intentionally unlike yours, about the only tolerable food, clothing, turns of speech, books, and music. They find humor in things you don't. They are like rude lodgers who join with their clansmen, speak their own language, and leave you out. One reason parents are intolerant of their teens' sullenness, their dismissal of wise parental counsel, and their loyalty to their awkward, unsteady friends is that they see it as rejection. It is rejection. And *it hurts*.

MEET FEAR WITH FAITH

Child psychologists often refer to parenting adolescents as walking a tightrope. Rabbi Nachman of Bratslav, the great Chassid, used a similar metaphor when he famously said, "All the world is a very narrow bridge. The main thing is not to be afraid." Raising a teenager is scary, and the only way to resist your fear is with *bitachon*, with faith: faith in your child and in your own parenting.

In both Judaism and adolescent psychology I found guidelines that have helped me as well as other parents keep the faith as our teens crossed the narrow bridge into adulthood. Accepting your teen does not mean that you should be indulgent or lax or permissive. It does mean that you understand both your teenager's strengths and limitations, her quirks and her awkward, two-steps-forward-one-step-back growth. It also means that you respect your teen's instinct to separate from you, and that even in his most foolhardy, rebellious moments, you find something about him to cherish.

HONOR YOUR TEEN'S NATURAL ABILITIES AND LIMITATIONS

We each possess a unique set of traits given to us by God at birth, and these include talents and strengths as well as weaknesses. I, for example, am so directionally impaired that I don't know my right hand from my left or on which side of an envelope to put the stamp without looking at a previously stamped envelope to guide me. I never learned my way around my college campus, can get lost driving from my home to my office (a half mile), and my memory (immediate recall and memory for faces) is in the tenth percentile. I have a deep and wide lack of knowledge of geography (a product of the spatial and memory impairment). On the other end of the curve, my vocabulary and reading comprehension are in the ninety-ninth percentile. I learn the lyrics to songs without effort, am a pretty good skier, and have been told many times that I have good comic timing as a public speaker. I'm a package deal: strengths and weaknesses. Our children are no different.

Faith in your child means studying her God-given traits, the good as well as the quirky, and working to cherish them. Your teen won't make this easy for you. Although teens are born with innate skills and temperaments, they are also constantly changing. They need to experiment with belonging to different tribes: pothead, slacker, mathlete, Wiccan, Emo, jock. One month they are vegans and the next they are training for an eating competition, hot dog division. They are growing into adulthood, but they are also ruder and cruder and sillier than they will ever be again. Amid all the phases and transitory passions, how do you spot your teen's essential nature?

I suggest looking back to your teen's infancy and childhood. Think about how you described your baby or child to their grandparents: Was she persistent and intense? Slow-paced? A "people person" or happier when alone? Funny? Energetic? Musical? Sensitive? Chances are these attributes still form a part of your teen's natural endowment. Although I don't recommend that you put your child in a glass jar labeled "the funny one" or "the smart one," it is wise to recognize that there are some characteristics that will not change. These include but are not limited to:

Musicality
Artistic inclination
Natural athletic talent
Taste in friends and romantic partners
Love of or indifference to reading
Speedy tempo or slow pace
Gregariousness or shyness
Preference for indoor versus outdoor activities
Attraction to risk and adventure or cautiousness

Recognizing your teen's temperament allows you to step back from our culture's narrow definition of success and see your child in her splendid uniqueness.

Letting your child relax into her true nature does not mean that you abandon your parental duties to protect, guide, and inspire. For example, you don't say, "Clearly an explorer/inventor/true poet/refined soul like you must feel trapped by the dull duties of everyday life, so blow off all your homework, skip your chores, catch the next bus out of town, and go seek creative fulfillment!" Nor do you say, "Because of your learning differences and sensitivity and very, very special needs, you are excused from the work the rest of us have to do." Instead, you balance your child's obligations with opportunities that match his ever-changing, emerging self. Allow your organized, slightly bossy child to quit chess club if he hates it, and let him take up the job of stage manager for the next choir production if that's where his heart lies. Don't confine your physically adventurous child indoors all weekend to study; let him ride a mountain bike or play paintball in the woods.

Honoring your child's temperament is an expression of *bitachon*. Our children belong to God and are made in God's image. Faith means believing that God doesn't make flawed merchandise. It means trusting that your child's innate attributes are proper and appropriate for them, that they are sufficient even for an uncertain future.

EXPECT YOUR CHILD TO DETOUR FROM THE BIG PLANS YOU'VE MADE

Be aware that recognizing your child's temperament requires more than just honoring his talents. You must be prepared for your child to put his talents to use in a way that disrupts all your carefully laid plans.

When I first met Ethan, he had recently received a report card of four C's and a D. At home he was savagely argumentative with his parents, and in school he was stoically miserable, refusing to hand in homework or speak in class unless spoken to. Ethan's parents were concerned and puzzled. Until now, their son had been an exceptional student. They'd spotted his aptitude for science in his early childhood and nurtured it carefully, encouraging him to take every science course available in their excellent public school system. In middle school, he breezed through pre-AP chemistry and physics without studying. Ethan's parents began to imagine their son as a doctor. This boy had serious intellectual capital; they would make certain he didn't squander it.

But in the course of therapy, Ethan's feelings emerged: He felt steam-rollered by his parents' ambitious plans. He'd wanted to take an art course in sculpture techniques, but his mother had pointed out the class conflicted with AP physics. Without AP physics his application to the best pre-med programs would be weak. His father said, "You can always take art classes, Ethan, but you can't take advanced science courses in college if you haven't had the basics." Ethan, not wanting to disappoint his parents, didn't argue. But he didn't work, either. Instead, he opted for what labor unions call "malicious compliance." He showed up at AP science and the rest of his classes, but he didn't participate or do the work.

When Ethan's parents realized that real respect for their son meant allowing him to use his gifts in a different direction, they set some restrictions on their own behavior. They put a moratorium on asking about grades. When Ethan asked for their opinion about which classes to take, they suggested that since his adviser at school knew the curriculum best, they trusted that he would offer good counsel. Ethan's parents also intentionally introduced subjects other than school into their conversations, talking about plans for putting in a new garden or a movie they had just seen. As Ethan felt his parents' fixation on his achievements fade, he developed the confidence to make independent decisions. That summer, instead of attending a prestigious summer math program, Ethan took a stagecraft workshop at the local state college. One day after class, he proudly showed his mother photos of an expansion bridge he was helping to design, complete with a massive Gorgon head at each entrance. "Look, Mom," he said, "this is science and math. But it's also *magic*. It's cool."

WHOSE PROBLEMS: THEIRS OR YOURS?

Taking a clear-eyed view of your teen's natural endowments also helps you stop confusing your own problems with your teen's. A woman named Melissa came to talk to me about her daughter, Molly, who was about fifteen pounds overweight. Melissa had been an overweight teen herself and was now what I call "white knuckle" slender—she spent a lot of time worrying about food and weighed herself first thing each morning. The numbers on the scale set her mood for the day. Molly's weight stirred up feelings of humiliation in her mother—Melissa said she felt that her private struggle was exposed by her daughter's appearance—but also great compassion as she remembered her own adolescent anguish. Melissa had been a shy girl who came home from school each day to have lunch with her lonely mother. Melissa responded to this memory of feeling lonely and ostracized by monitoring Molly's food intake and nagging her to lose the extra pounds.

But as we discovered together, Molly was a wholly different character from her mother. She was exuberant and popular, engaged in many activities. Her weight did not seem to hold her back from anything. When Melissa realized that Molly was not suffering the way she did, she stopped nagging and fussing. In recognizing that her daughter had a temperament different from her own, Melissa found more composure. She felt grateful that her daughter, unlike so many of her classmates, was not tyrannized by the belief that in order to be happy she needed to deny herself the hearty pleasures of life.

EXPECT IMMATURITY

Acceptance of teenagers goes past acceptance of their innate personality traits. It also means accepting that they are still developing. They're not fully cooked yet. It's not fair to expect them to act like young adults when, from a neurological and psychological perspective, they are still children.

Case in point: Luke was sixteen years old when his mother, Jody, who had not gone on a trip by herself since she had children, went to Paris for two weeks to visit a friend. Jody brought home a small, elegant box of chocolates with pictures of French landmarks delicately etched on top. On the flight home, Jody imagined the sweet moment when Luke would hold the chocolates up one by one and ask, "Did you go here? Did you go there? What was it like? And how do you pronounce this: Luxem*burg* or Luxem*bourg*?"

But it didn't go as she imagined. Luke did not say, "Mom, how was your trip?" or "What did you bring me?" or " Oh, chocolates! How kind and thoughtful of you. Boy, how I missed you, Mom" or even "Hi." On the day Jody returned from Paris, Luke walked in the door from school and said, "Can I take your car? I'm going to Tessa's." Later, he ate all the chocolates without comment. When Jody inquired about this spectacular lack of greeting and lack of graciousness about her gift, Luke said, "I didn't remember that you were away. And I didn't notice the decorations on the chocolates before I ate them." And this was true: He didn't and he hadn't.

Jody was furious at her son. Did he lack feelings? Had she raised a person with poor character? How would he function as an adult with flaws like these? None of Luke's teachers ever complained about his decorum in school, but on a day-to-day basis Luke was not particularly polite to his parents or his sister. Nor did he show any signs of having missed Jody. His mother was gone for two weeks, and he was *fine*.

There was nothing wrong with Luke. Teens may look like adults, but on the inside they are still under construction. Over the past twenty years, neuroscientists have learned that the teenage brain radically changes its structure in adolescence. There is a beautiful scientific term for the process of brain development that occurs between age ten and puberty: *exuberance.* This period of vigorous production of brain cells is followed, between the ages of fourteen and seventeen, by a period of pruning them back, when the gray matter thins dramatically. The brain becomes more streamlined and efficient. But the frontal lobes, the areas of the brain responsible for rationality and modulation of impulses and desires, do not reach full development for girls until age twenty-four or twenty-five and for boys until age twenty-nine. Judgment and wisdom, or, in the language of the neuropsychologists, *executive functions,* live in the part of the brain that is last to mature.

Luke was not neurologically developed enough yet to think, *It is not only polite but in my best interests to greet my mother after a long trip.* In an adult, Luke's behavior might be a red flag for pathological narcissism or sociopathy. In a teen, it was evidence of normal neurological immaturity. I often say to worried parents, "If you think of your teen as ping-ponging between the ages of five and thirty-five, his behavior won't seem so odd." An accepting parent tries to guide a child toward great maturity, but tries not to panic at immature behavior, or take it too personally, or mistake it for a permanent character flaw.

Powerful brain scans or studies are compelling, but we don't really need them to tell us that teenagers suffer from what Shakespeare long ago identified as "boiled brains." They are moody, impulsive, drawn to risk, disorganized, and vain. I'll bet you are not currently drawn to high-speed amusement park rides or beer pong or driving fast at night with the lights off, but you did your version of these things when you were a teenager, and your children have to do some version of them, too. The same goes for storing completed homework assignments under a damp towel on the floor of the bedroom, or weeping in anguish over a new haircut that to your eyes looks exactly the same as the style they've always had. If you confront teens with their bizarre behavior and ask, "What were you thinking?" the usual answers are:

Nothing.

I thought it would be fun. And it was.

It's fine, Mom. There's a tank top underneath the towel that keeps my home-work dry.

I didn't think Aunt Jane would see my Facebook wall.

I can't go to school with my hair like this. I look like the wrong kind of person.

Or, as in the case of Luke (a boy who loves and respects his mother), *I didn't say a big hello because I didn't remember that you were gone.*

In the world of teenagers, being spacey is normal. Lack of imagination about the consequences of one's actions is normal. Shifting enthusiasms are normal. Terrible boredom with you is normal. Your child's conviction that it is a tragedy of earth-shattering proportions that she has been born into the wrong family (so strict! so boring! so ordinary! so lacking in compassion!) is normal. Your daughter's endless dramas and urgent demands are normal. Your son's preoccupation with food fights and barfing is normal. Your child sullenly reminding you that Natalie and Natasha and Nora all have parents who are more understanding and cooler than you are is normal.

We have to permit our children time to develop and grow. Unfortunately, we're usually inclined to do the opposite. Try to remember that teens aren't fully grown yet. They may not become their full adult selves until they are twenty-five . . . or thirty-seven.

GAIN PERSPECTIVE ON THE COLLEGE ADMISSIONS FRENZY

You can study your teenager's temperament, and you can accept the ups and downs of adolescent development, but unless you can disengage from the college admissions frenzy, you will find it difficult to allow your child to bloom in his own way, on his own schedule. You'll be too caught up in the belief that every choice your child makes, starting around age twelve, will be reflected on the all-important college application.

It's true that the world has changed since you and I were young. Middle school is more academically rigorous, high school is harder, and college admissions are more competitive. But our generation's particular challenge as parents is to acknowledge this reality without exaggerating it. Let's start with the myth that only students who attend the most selective, highest-in-the-*U.S. News*-poll schools can achieve real success. In his 2004 *Atlantic* article "Who Needs Harvard?" Greg Easterbrook cites admissions officers who believe that there are about a hundred colleges that deliver the same quality education as what Easterbrook calls the top-of-the-list "glamour" schools. He also describes a 1999 study, conducted by Alan Krueger of Princeton and Stacy Berg Dale of the Andrew Mellon Foundation, of students who were accepted at Ivy League schools but chose to go elsewhere because of better financial aid packages, a location closer to home, or other advantages. Twenty years after graduation, these students made as much money as their Ivy League peers.

Lloyd Thacker, the author of *College Unranked,* is a former college admissions officer and the founder of the Education Conservancy, a nonprofit organization with the mission of restoring sanity to the college application process. Its motto? "Collectively we have robbed students of their senior year." Thacker says it is the *student* who contributes most significantly to the educational payoff, not the college. The most reliable predictors of adult success are not grades in high school or a collegiate pedigree. They are the qualities that psychologist Daniel Goleman calls emotional intelligence: empathy, optimism, flexibility, a good sense of humor, the capacity to function as a team member, and a positive reaction to setbacks.

One teaching that resonated with readers of *The Blessing of a Skinned Knee* is the Chassidic proverb "If your child has talent to be a baker, don't ask him to be a doctor." Your child needs a post–high school experience that is a good fit for his temperament, needs, and talents. You want him to explore his interests, form supportive friendships, and stretch toward maturity. This means accepting that your child might actually want to be a baker, not a business whiz, and to go to cooking school, not Stanford.

STOP MEASURING AND COMPARING

Our society measures teenagers at every turn: Are you good? Better? Best? What's your rank? Shall we select you or reject you? What will you major in? Music. Music and what else?

Even for kids who rank at the top of every field and are accepted to the college of their choice, this brutal measurement process feels like the opposite of acceptance. It tells them they are only as good as their last test score. By constantly criticizing our teens, we send the message that we, too, are constantly measuring and comparing.

Sometimes the best way to show acceptance of your teen is to bite your tongue. Try not to pollute interactions with your teen with constant suggestions for improvement:

Yes, a B plus is fine. But remember, I suggested that highlighting the book and making a written outline might have been a better approach.

Did you know that twenty minutes of aerobic exercise every day significantly enhances brain function?

You've got another paper coming up next week, so consider getting started a bit earlier this time . . . and, by the way, too many carbs can make you sleepy.

Instead, let affirmation—"Yes, a B plus!"—stand happily alone.

Some parents sneak in criticism by disguising it as encouragement, by upping the ante every time their child does something well. This is the "What about varsity?" school of parenting. If the child is a good listener, we encourage her to join the school peer support team. If she makes second chair in the orchestra, we suggest that next year she aim for first. If he plays a team sport at school, why not move up to a club sport? If junior varsity, why not go all the way?

Perhaps the best and most radical way to stop measuring and comparing your teen is to keep yourself from mentioning college before the eleventh grade. Clench your teeth if you have to. Every year at the back-to-school night for parents of tenth graders at the Oakwood School in Los Angeles, dean Erin Studer gives the parents two messages: "Don't talk about college this year *at all,* and remember, they aren't very good drivers yet even if they have a license." I agree.

TREASURE YOUR HOMELY, HOLY TEEN

The Jewish holiday of Sukkot commemorates the Israelites' long, hard trip through the desert after leaving Egypt. To prepare for the festivities, each family heads out to the backyard or apartment balcony and builds a sukkah, a rickety hut resembling the makeshift desert shelters of the Israelites. In a nightly ritual, each person waves around a long, graceful cluster of palm, laurel, and myrtle fronds while cradling a funny-looking, thick-skinned, bumpy, yellow citrus fruit called an etrog.

If you want a real spiritual lesson during Sukkot, think of the etrog as your teenager. The etrog is misshapen and expensive, but one of the pleasures of Sukkot is the love you show it. Even the word itself, *etrog*, is Aramaic for "delight." Each family takes great care in selecting the proper etrog, which can cost between ten and one thousand dollars. (It's true. Ask a rabbi.) Then you bring your etrog home, swaddled in fluffy batting in a simple white cardboard box. During the weeklong holiday, the family performs a ritual in the sukkah, saying prayers to thank God for the miracle of the Exodus, the gathering of the family, and the cycle of festivals. My favorite moment is when the family opens the box holding the etrog. Everyone looks in and says, "Oh, it's beautiful!" You speak the words while battling a strong sense of cognitive dissonance, since you just spent forty dollars on a lemon, but also with genuine love for a religious tradition that gets you out of the house and involved in such serious, holy silliness.

Every etrog is homely, and every etrog is cherished and elevated and given a starring role for a whole week, every year, every place in the world where Jews celebrate their holidays. You don't need to wave palm fronds at your teen. But there is value in cherishing her not just for who she was as an infant or for what she will one day become, but for what she is now, in all her lumpy, bumpy glory.

As a spiritual exercise, try to cultivate appreciation for your teen—not just for what you find easy to love about her, but for what you don't. What are the most upsetting signs of her rejection of you, of her clannishness with her friends, of her immaturity? Her taste in music might be a good place to begin. Remember when you had to read daunting classics in high school or college but found, to your surprise, that after fifty pages you were inhabiting the author's world and delighting in it, that you had found the rhythm and beauty? Treat your teen's music as the curriculum for a three-hundred-level course in Modern American Song. Ask her to play it softly for you or to download the lyrics so you can read them while you listen. Find the emotion, the social commentary, the irony, the playfulness, and joy in the music. (Aquabats! Even the name is fun.) You don't have to pretend you love it. Just listen with an open mind, curiosity, and consideration.

What about your teen's tribal attire? I can guarantee that by the time you read this the styles will have changed, but right now the group called "scene kids" who hang out at the Guitar Center near my house favor choppy, very black hair, often covering one eye; fingerless gloves; white leather belts; T-shirts bearing images of dinosaurs and robots; and, for some, septum piercing (you've seen this; toward the bottom of the nose, like a little sow). You have a right as a parent to be appalled by your child's taste in fashion—or to prohibit permanent disfiguration, as in piercings. But remember that God asks us to treasure even the strangest fruits. Say to yourself: *Isn't it interesting that teen tribes like the scene kids have strict rules and standards, but that they also make playful, colorful, and original combinations—like fingerless gloves and dinosaurs on your T-shirt? When else in life does a person get to do this?*

Or try looking at teenaged moodiness, so wearying to parents, from a different perspective. Teens are frequently upset because so much is deeply valuable to them. Their idealism reflects ideals. They feel indignation and anger because they hold the values of rights and justice dear; their hysteria over a pimple or a bad-hair day or the need for the exactly, perfectly correct style of jeans reflects their ideal of beauty. They feel almost unendurable anguish over a rejection or break-up or exclusion from their social group because they care so deeply about loyalty and relationships. They appear lazy because they value rest and relaxation; they chafe at rules because they value freedom; they play their music so loudly because they *love their music so much.*

I don't suggest that you jump into a mosh pit with your child, or buy your clothes where she does, or that you vibrate with her every emotion. If you do that, you're not acting like a parent; you are acting like a creepy, middle-aged friend. But it is reassuring to teens when their parents can see beauty amid the pain of their transformation. Look for occasions when you can truthfully and specifically praise your teen, not just for her potential, but for what she is right now:

I like how your pigtails go with your cowgirl outfit.

I see why you like the ukulele. It has such a happy sound that I can't help smiling every time I hear you play.

Thanks for taking Phillip along with you to the movies. He told me he had a great time.

Fantastic. I would have no idea how to pull together a CD mix like that.

Life with teens will be more fun for you if you can derive at least some entertainment value from the experience. *Baruch atah Adonai elohaynu melech ha-olam m'shaneh ha-briot* is the Hebrew prayer you say when you see an exceptionally beautiful or funny-looking person or animal. It means, "Thank you, God, for varying the creatures." You don't always have to mean it or believe it. But you can think of it as a mantra for parents who are learning to accept and appreciate the exotic creatures their teenage children have become.

CHAPTER 3

The Blessing of a Bad Attitude:

Living Graciously with the Chronically Rude

Nancy, a single mother, is telling me about Theo, her wildly accomplished son. He's a high school junior, a biathlete, the top biology student in his grade, an award-winning nature photographer . . . and, in her eyes, an arrogant sourpuss:

He's so rude. Last week I woke up early to make him a special breakfast: chocolate chip pancakes. And he just stared down at the plate and said, "You know I don't eat this junk." Then he pulled out a Clif bar from the kitchen cabinet and ate it on his way out the door. He didn't even say good-bye.

But at least that morning he was awake! Usually he oversleeps. I bought him two alarm clocks. One is called the Sonic Boom. It shakes the whole house. The other is on wheels and rolls away when the alarm rings so you have to get out of bed to turn it off. But he doesn't get up. What am I supposed to do? Let him miss first period? I usually have to shake him awake, and then he yells, "Get out of my room!"

I don't know what to say when he's so awful. Growing up, I would have never treated my parents like this.

There was a time when a young person rose when an adult entered the room, would not consider calling adults by their first names, and automatically came to the door to pick up a date. I am not nostalgic for this time. Socially acceptable behavior also included discrimination of every sort, sweeping family problems under the rug, and establishing household order through intimidation and submissive deference to Dad the All-Knowing Patriarch.

Most parents I see want to raise their teens with greater compassion and sensitivity than they received while growing up. As a result, our children are chattier, cozier, and more direct with us—and they are also ruder. As adolescence sets in and they are driven to separate from us, they push us away with their attitude, behavior, and facial expressions. They say "I hate you!" or "I don't care what you think!" Sometimes they call us names. Within reasonable limits, these are exasperating but healthy signs of our more open, relaxed relationships. Our children feel confident that they can perform the painful work of weaning themselves from Mom and Dad without losing our love. Which leaves today's parents with a dilemma: How do we respect our teenagers' need to separate from us while fulfilling our parental duty to teach them respect for others?

It *is* a duty, and a sacred one. Respect for others is at the core of Jewish teachings. The great Rabbi Hillel was once asked, "If you could teach all of Judaism while standing on one foot, what would you say?" Hillel responded, "Treat your neighbors as yourself." Always, Judaism stresses deed before creed. Your actions, not your beliefs, are the true measure of your character. This is one reason God gave us laws—the 613 mitzvot that cover every aspect of life, especially mutual kindness. Some examples: We are required to give charity according to our means. We may not withhold an employee's wages beyond payday. We must not muzzle an ox who is threshing in corn it can eat and enjoy. Farmers must leave an unreaped corner of the field for the poor. Judaism teaches that whether a person is considerate of others is as important as whether he prays daily. We are the sum of our actions, and most of our actions are small deeds, not large gestures.

Torah teaches us that parents are God's holy stand-ins. This means that parents are responsible for placing respect and consideration at the center of the family mission. They need to devote as much attention, intelligence, and sensitivity to their teen's treatment of others as they do to their child's schooling or health. Ideally, parents will teach their children to be compassionate without becoming martyrs, to be forthright without being obnoxious.

How, then, does a compassionate parental leader teach respect? A successful strategy for teaching respect involves what may feel like an inhuman amount of levelheaded patience, tolerance, and serenity on your part. You have to let teens do their work of separation while knowing that they are keenly studying your every move. They will learn more than you can imagine by watching how you define the standards of respect that matter most to you; by your thoughtful, authoritative reaction when they inevitably challenge those standards; and by your own practice of generosity toward them, even when they don't deserve it.

HOW RUDE IS TOO RUDE?

Teens are most likely to engage in egregious rudeness—insulting, cursing, slamming doors—when your expectations of them are either inappropriate or unclear. Overly strict expectations, with no room for the emotional inexperience of adolescence, will backfire. If you expect your teen to *never* roll her eyes at you or melt down after a bad day at school, you will find yourself criticizing and nagging constantly, and your teen will withdraw or rebel or take her behavior underground.

But fuzzy expectations are just as bad. Remember that teens depend on you to be strong. If they sense that you don't really know what you want, they will feel insecure. Then they'll push at you even harder—with more insults, more arrogance, more seemingly pointless conflict. A clear, thoughtful, calm parental stance is reassuring to them. For your own clarity of mind, I suggest you develop some reasonable minimum standards for polite behavior in your home. This task begins with a look at your family's style and your teen's temperament.

No set list of behaviors is appropriate for all families and teens. Some families are like a genre of youth music called "scream-o," in which the lead singer screams in a wildly loud, hoarse voice over an electronic background. (Try listening to the band I Set My Friends on Fire.) If the music doesn't scare you off immediately, it becomes strange and appealing, like a pep rally in hell. "Scream-o" families are energetic and loud, shouting their way to compromise. The surface is rough but underneath there's melody, love, and commitment. In other families, no one raises their voice. Even calling loudly from downstairs to come to dinner is not acceptable. Some families tease and spar verbally, by calling each other names. Others are physical and wrestle and tussle. Still others are quiet and tender. There's no proper tempo or template for good manners for every family.

The family style may get shaken up when your child reaches adolescence. Now one person in the "loud" family is withdrawn (Are his silences or one-word replies rude?); one person in the decorous family grows raucous (Is his noise and boisterousness rude?); one in the competitive family becomes sensitive (Is her prickliness fussy and self-absorbed?); one in the physical family finds touching intrusive (Is she cold and rejecting?). It's a challenge to determine what is reasonable when one person in a family changes.

You might find it easier to identify standards for your family by looking elsewhere, by studying your reaction to other families. When you are out in public, watch the teens, both in groups and with their parents. What impresses you as mature behavior? Is it the teen who invites a loner cousin to join the dancing at a bar mitzvah? Who paces herself to a frail grandparent's gait? Who shakes your hand when leaving your house and says, "Thank you for having me"? And what do you see that troubles you most? The teen who talks back to a parent in public? Continues eating or chewing while being introduced to an adult? Who plays drums in the garage after nine o'clock on a school night? Bring these ideas back to your own home and compare them to the temperament of your family and teen. Be prepared to adjust your list over time, as your teen matures or—as teens tend to do—temporarily regresses.

When my girls entered adolescence, I drew up a mental list of behaviors that I considered out of bounds. Know that your list can and should be different.

You might consider it rude if your teenager:

- Curses directly at you or other family members
- Insults you in front of others
- Doesn't answer other people's direct questions
- Stays out past curfew (this one fits the category of creating a situation where others will worry)
- Slams doors frequently
- Breaks things without apologizing, repairing, or replacing them
- Is unwilling to make polite small talk with parents' friends
- Uses your stuff without asking
- Goes into sibling's room without permission
- Changes the radio station in the car without asking you

Here's a list of behaviors that are also rude but that I chose to ignore so that my daughters and I weren't fighting all the time.

You might choose to ignore:

- Sullenness/sulking
- Grousing before chores, homework, required tasks
- Eyeball rolling
- Grunting
- Occasional lack of greetings: "Good morning, Mom," "Bye, Dad"
- Frequent but mild teasing, arguing, and fighting with siblings
- Slamming doors from time to time
- Cursing in front of, but not directly at, a parent
- Staying out a half hour past curfew on occasion because of extenuating circumstances
- Treating the stuff you buy them in a careless manner (it's theirs now but you don't have to buy them more)
- Using an impolite tone of voice with friends or discussing profane topics with them
- Getting mad at you for irrational reasons
- Giving you the "scram eyes" when a friend is over

What good is making such a list? It helps you figure out where you stand, so you won't have to constantly second-guess yourself about whether you are asking too much or too little of your teen. Also, having clearly defined standards protects you from being buffeted about by other influences. This way, when your teen inevitably complains that you are too strict:

Mom, everyone I know tells their parents to go to hell now and then.

You won't be as likely to give in—and then regret it later.

When your own parents complain that you are too lenient:

You know you're spoiling those kids, don't you?

You'll be less tempted to spin into a confused reevaluation of every single parenting decision you've ever made. Having a list lets you operate with greater confidence. Edit and revise the list as needed.

There isn't one best way to respond to behavior you have determined is unacceptably rude. How you deal with it depends on the cause—and to understand the most common causes of rudeness, let's take a look into the heart and mind of your mercurial, indelicate teen.

WHY NICE CHILDREN HAVE TO BECOME RUDE TEENAGERS

What happened to your sweet five-year-old, the one who planned to marry you when she grew up and said things like "You are the most beautiful, bestest Mommy in the whole wide world?" Did someone take her in the night? This new child, this changeling, acts aloof, uncaring, bitchy. She says, "Clearly you don't understand me . . . or anything else," or "I can't take one more day of living in this family!" But it's not personal. In addition to separating from you—which she does in her inexperienced, clumsy manner—there are several ways that her rudeness is developmentally normal and even an instinct toward growth.

It's All About Me

"Decentering" is the term psychologist Jean Piaget uses to describe the capacity to take another person's point of view. Technically, this ability kicks in at around age six or seven and is developed by about age twelve, but when a teenager is stressed, tired, or anxious, her thinking becomes less mature. In trying circumstances, decentering is one of the first cognitive skills to go. When teens say things like:

Please don't volunteer to chaperone the school trip. Not if you're going to wear that ponytail.

I'm not eating this. It looks like dog food.

Don't look at me. Don't talk to me.

They aren't decentering. They aren't thinking about the impact of their behavior or the implications of their words on *you* (your self-consciousness about your hair, your cooking skill, your parental worthiness); they are telling you about *themselves* (their easy embarrassment, their finicky and rapidly changing teenage palate, their low mood at that moment). Depending on their maturity and the intensity of the offensive comment, you might just let it pass. Or, in an even voice, let them know that they are crossing the lines set by civilized society: "That's unkind, Meghan," or "Whoa, not okay to talk to me that way." The tried-and-true technique of "I" statements can also come in handy: "When you use the words 'dinner' and 'dog food' in the same sentence, I'm annoyed because I worked hard to prepare this meal in hopes that you would like it." "When you insult my appearance, I'm surprised and hurt." Then briskly move on to a different subject . . . or a different room.

Rudeness as Relief

Teens also use rudeness to blow off steam. Remember how your small children marched off to preschool, followed all the rules, sat in a circle at circle time, used their inside voices, put their lunch boxes back in the cubby, raised their hands to speak, held it together all day long—and then fell apart when you picked them up? Teenagers, in a second toddlerhood, do the same thing. They are required to be courteous to the most irritating, boring teacher and to the PE instructor who yells at them if they can't complete their laps around the track; and if they are starting middle or high school they are once again the little fishes. Like the frustrated office worker who can't take it out on the boss, they come home and kick the cat: you—a safe target—because they know you love them and they trust you not to retaliate. The difference between the screechy tantrum of a four-year-old and the insult hurled by a fourteen-year-old is that one hurts your ears and the other hurts your feelings. Some days it takes all your parental resolve not to kick them back.

But you can't kick them back, not if you want them to feel that you are safely in control of your emotions. If your teen yells, "Shut up!" at you and runs into her room, locking the door behind her, you may be tempted to march up to the door and bang on it, shouting, "Young lady, you will not talk to me that way!"

By reacting emotionally to your teen's provocation, you lose your position of authority. Instead, respond calmly. If your teen's rudeness hits you in a sore spot, like a childhood memory of being bossed around or bullied, give yourself a breather. Take a few of those deep, cleansing breaths one learns in yoga class. Try saying, "It's hard to have a conversation when you are speaking in that tone of voice. Let's start over." Even if your teen storms off, you've set your minimum parameters for communication. And *you* are welcome to walk away from a teen whose behavior is inflammatory. Depending on the circumstances, you might approach your child later, saying, "You seemed pretty stressed when you came home this afternoon. Any new developments at school today?" You might not get a substantive answer, but at least you've established that you, the parent, are available to listen to the problems that lie beneath the rudeness.

Rudeness as a Canny Maneuver

You can eat, live, buy, and do whatever you please. Teenagers have very few choices, even when they have lots of privileges. They're prisoners in a house they didn't pick, in a town they didn't pick, with parents they didn't pick. Because their perception of time is so different from ours, they imagine they'll be enslaved forever. Besides parent-approved ways to feel powerful (do well in school, do well in sports, be a leader), the easiest ways for them to test their strength are to play pranks or to be rowdy or defiant. When they tell you they're sleeping at Olivia's when they're really at Jake's, they're using a shortcut to freedom. The best way for them to fight back if they are caught is to yell, issue withering sarcastic remarks, or shift the blame by insulting you.

Since they study you, they know how to deftly target your vulnerability. Their words can sting. Take these three examples, in ascending degree of sophistication, each told to me by parents of fourteen-year-old girls:

Daughter: *Mom, I'm sleeping at Charlotte's house tonight.*
  Mom: *Sorry, but you need a good night's sleep tonight. You have an early game tomorrow.*
Daughter: *You know what? I sleep better at Charlotte's than at home. I hate you. You're a terrible mother.*

Dad, the reason you won't let me go to the mall with my friends is that everyone knows you weren't very popular with the babes when you were in high school. This doesn't mean it's fair to keep me in solitary confinement.

Mom, the reason you're so strict and make such bizarre rules is because you have a lot of personal problems. [dramatic pause]
And everyone we know knows this about you. [another dramatic pause]
And they talk about it all the time.

(Note how two of the teens use a version of the phrase "everyone knows." Everyone does not know. This is merely a ploy to unbalance you and weaken your conviction so they can get what they want.)

If your teen uses rudeness as an attack on your rules, and *you* respond heatedly, it will seem as if you've pulled out your sword for a duel and dared them to pull out theirs:

Go ahead, sleep at Charlotte's. Live at Charlotte's if you want to. You're the one who wanted to be on the team. Good, skip the game. Then I can sleep late and be relieved of the burden of driving you across town in the morning.

Who wins when you escalate the battle? They do, because you've just been successfully distracted from the real issue, which is the rule you are setting or enforcing. You'll have more success if you ignore the attack and stay focused on your mission, which is enforcing the rule at hand.

Start or end your response with one of these words, or make them the whole sentence:

Nevertheless . . .
Regardless . . .
That is not the issue.
My decision is final.
I've thought about it and my answer is no.
I remember saying no about this.
I'm not going to change my mind about this.
I'm not ready for that movie . . . coed sleepover . . . computer in your room.

(Observe that the emphasis is on *your* readiness, not your child's, so you don't invite debate.)

It can feel irresponsible, even dangerous, to ignore a teen's insults, but the technique works. Use it enough, and your teen will learn that rudeness is not an effective way to get around your rules. If you can enforce your rules with your teenagers without struggling to reach a consensus or getting trapped in a back-and-forth battle, there is a bonus: You are providing a model for them to do the same with their friends. For instance, your teenager might say, "No, I'm not going to stay at this party, I'm going to call my dad to pick me up—and no, I'm not going to keep explaining why."

They Don't Know What to Do with Strong Feelings

Even when teens are not being rude, their emotions are intense, and they don't have any experience managing their new range of strong feelings. Younger children can get very, very angry, or feel crushed by embarrassment, but teens travel in new, more complex emotional territory. They are experiencing unfamiliar combinations of emotional states—grief, joy, frustration, agitation—and since you are the person who lives with them, they practice working through these emotions on you. It's surprising to some parents to hear me say, "Teenagers are entitled to a private relationship with their deep feelings, and it's not your job to try to make those feelings go away. Their emotions are theirs, not yours. This is a silver lining of separation: You don't have to feel what your teenager feels."

Ideally, your teen should be able to come to you in a bad mood, see that you are compassionate but not terribly concerned, and then go away again—even if she goes away to wallow in her misery for a while. This tells her that however wild and out of control she feels, you remain solid. This practice is very similar to the one you used when your child played in the park: They ran to you and touched you and then ran off again, reassured that Mom or Dad was still there. If your teen comes to you in a bad mood and you get upset because she's upset, or you start diagnosing her, fixing the problem, or getting impatient, you are no longer her home base. She won't feel safe enough to come back to you with her troubles next time.

One overlooked reason parents get so rattled by teenagers' rough manners and rudeness is that their behavior comes in such a big or tall or verbally adroit package. It's easy to forget they are not adults. When they were little and said, "I hate you, stupid Mommy! I wish I could hit you with a thousand stones," it was cute because it was coming out of a cute package. When they're big and say, "You're a sad, pathetic human being," it's hard to feel tickled. If an actual adult spoke to us that way, we would either be very scared or very angry. A trick to help you tolerate teenage rudeness is to mentally shrink them down. Imagine how they looked when they were five years old and wearing floaties or a sparkly tutu or a superhero Halloween costume. When they are flooded with emotion or frustration, they are a lot closer in maturity to that child than they are to being a seasoned adult. They still need you to be steady so they can learn how to steady themselves.

WHY ARE THEY NICE TO EVERYONE BUT ME?

When I meet with parents to size up a teen's need for testing, therapy, or some other kind of psychological help, I always ask what the teachers have to say about the child and if he has any friends. I'm surprised by how frequently the parents smile and shake their heads up and down: "Oh, teachers like him a lot, he has plenty of friends, nice ones, too, but he is horrible. I don't know why they put up with him."

I do. He's fair and thoughtful and fun with his friends, in a teenagey way. "Hey, asshole, feeling better today? It sucked sitting through Geometry without you." And he's probably decent to his teachers or coaches, too. Ever watch tadpoles develop into frogs? There's a point near the very end when they've got their froggy hands and legs but their fish tail is still attached. They can sit on a rock, breathing air, but they have to keep their tiny tadpole tail in the water. You are that water. When your child uses reasonably good manners with other adults while at home he is standoffish, loud, touchy, demanding, and lacking in gratitude (particularly with his mother), it can be wrenching, but it's a sign that adolescence is progressing normally. On the other hand, if you get complaints that your child behaves badly to other adults, or if his nice friends have dropped him, then it's time to seek outside help. A counselor or therapist experienced in working with teenagers and their families can assist you and your child in unearthing the causes of his self-destructive behavior.

DOUBLE-MINDEDNESS AS PARENTING STRATEGY

One day your teen's hormones will stabilize and her brain will mature. As she eventually earns more freedom and rights, she will feel less frustrated. In time, she will naturally begin to see you as a person with feelings and needs. She will decenter. Remember Theo? I am confident that one day Theo will enter the kitchen, give Nancy a kiss, and say something like, "Remember how you used to make me those chocolate chip pancakes? I loved them so much. How about we make some again for old times' sake?" (That day, however, may be a *very* long time coming.) As one grandmother I know put it, "One day your teenager will emerge from her bedroom, walk down the stairs, and be surprised at how reasonable her parents have become."

It is critical for you not to get lost in the fear that your teen's rudeness is a permanent moral flaw. If you do, you will not have the presence of mind to remain tolerant and calm. This is a good time to ponder what *bitachon,* trust in God, means to you. When parents confide that they feel uncomfortable with the "G word," I sometimes suggest that they substitute the word "reality": I believe in reality. I trust in reality. I honor reality. My child is made in reality's image. It is a developmental reality that babies learn to crawl and walk. It is a developmental reality that teenagers eventually learn to connect to a world outside of their immediate desires.

But although you must have faith in the eternal forces of time and maturation, you cannot depend on time and maturation *alone.* Teens need your feedback so they can learn where the boundaries of good behavior are located. Remember when your teenager was a toddler and dropped the sippy cup over and over again from the high chair, delighting in the clatter when it hit the floor? Your baby was studying the properties of velocity and physics. Now your teenager is studying comparative ethics. He's learning about community standards and mutual respect by taking the whole apparatus apart and tinkering with the pieces. Your teen needs your help understanding the social order, to explain: "This is one of those rules that carries grave consequences if you break it. And *this* is a rule that is more flexible, but not infinitely so." If you let things get out of hand, your teen may be too rude to be accepted into civilized society, or even to garner the most basic goodwill from you.

WHEN HEALTHY RUDENESS BECOMES CONTEMPT

Parents who want to reduce conflict with their surly children often start by criticizing themselves. I'm thinking again of Nancy, who turned out to be as angry with herself as she was with Theo. "I'm chronically irritable with him," she told me. "I nag him to use good manners, I yell and create an unpleasant atmosphere in the house. Why can't I relax?"

"In this situation I don't particularly care about Theo," I said. "I care that this is a lousy way to start *your* day. It is unpleasant *for you*." Far from acting like the head of the house, Nancy was acting more like Dobby, the house elf in the Harry Potter books. She complained, she pouted, she occasionally threw a fit, but she did not assert her authority by laying down some clear parameters for her son's morning responsibilities and for his treatment of her in general. Theo sensed her self-doubt, and he played it to his advantage. "He's a satisfied frustrater," I told Nancy, "and you are a frustrated satisfier."

Yes, as the parent of a teen, you will have to tolerate behavior that would be unacceptable at any other point or in any other area in your life. I have asked you to meet your teen's rudeness with equanimity. But there is a limit. Your home should not become a site of everyday ugliness and parent abuse. I often say to parents who are worn down by their teens' constant verbal assaults, "You work hard, you pay the bills, you drive your kids around to their activities, you schedule their doctor's appointments, you go to the grocery store, you give them thoughtful advice, and you receive little appreciation for any of it. Because of all the work you do, it's important for your home to be a relatively peaceful place where you can relax and take refuge from the work of the day."

I tell parents who are frustrated by persistent rudeness about the concept of *shalom bayit,* peace in the home. According to Jewish teachings, maintaining *shalom bayit* is your responsibility, and enjoying *shalom bayit* is your right. It's a matter of both your comfort and your dignity. A house in which teenagers routinely slam their bedroom doors, destroy the peace by shouting, or respond to invitations to eat dinner with the family by saying, "I told you to leave me alone," is not a haven.

Your list of unacceptably rude behaviors will help you determine whether your teen suffers from developmentally normal rudeness or whether he's got a case of insensitivity and disrespect that makes *shalom bayit* impossible. If the items on your Too Rude list are consistently violated, you have work to do.

Use your list to create standards of respect for the household and lay down specific ground rules. One or two new rules is the most you can expect a teenager to process at any one time, so think about what disturbs you the most. Is it the rudeness itself? Or is it a situation that predictably leads to everyone getting angry and upset, such as Theo's refusal to wake up for school on time? Keeping in mind that teenagers have the right to strong negative feelings, concentrate on behaviors rather than attitudes:

When you arrive home from school, I expect you to say a brief "hi" so I know you're here.

It's your job to wake yourself up in the morning by seven o'clock.

You know we don't mind occasional cursing, but you may not call us names.

Don't try to introduce new rules in the heat of a conflict. Wait, and have a family conversation when the involved parties are feeling relatively rested, fed, and unhurried. (You may be thinking, *And when would that be?* The key word is "relatively.") Or, if your child tends to get defensive or withdraws when faced by both parents, discuss the rules one-on-one. Once you have clearly explained the behavior that bothers you and why, brainstorm ways to solve the problem. If your child has a solution she is enthusiastic about, consider giving it a try even if it seems far-fetched:

If you put a sticker on the back doorknob, it'll remind me to say hi to you when I walk in.

Or repugnant:

I can get ready for school on time if I just sleep in my clothes for the next day.

Or foolish:

I can wake up on my own at seven-fifteen because my friend Whitney is going to call me on my cell phone every day.

Or likely to create new problems:

If I'm not ready on time, I won't expect you to drive me. I'll walk and get a tardy.

These solutions may be effective simply because your child thought of them herself. This creates an element of "buy in" from the start. If several ideas are on the table, discuss the pros and cons of each and allow your teen to choose one of them. (You have veto power over proposals that are patently unacceptable, but use that power with restraint.) Then determine how the outcome will be measured and—this is important— the gratifying changes that will take place when success is consistently achieved. In *The Blessing of a Skinned Knee* I talked about using the formula "when . . . then " for encouraging young children to cooperate with adults. It works with teenagers as well: "When you consistently remember on your own to (get up on time, bring drinking glasses from your room to the kitchen and put them in the dishwasher, call if you change your plans midstream) then we will be happy to (consider giving you a later curfew, give you a larger allowance, let you drive to the beach with your friends). You will have shown us you are responsible."

If success is not achieved, what are appropriate consequences? They'll be different for each family, but they always begin at the same place: the borderline between entitlements and privileges. Like young children, teenagers are entitled to respectful treatment, healthful food, shelter from the elements, practical and comfortable clothing, checkups at the doctor and dentist, and a good education. Everything else is a privilege. Any privilege may be withheld by you until a specified behavioral standard has been met. Once you've agreed on incentives and measurable standards for acceptable behavior, make sure you hold up your end of the deal. If your teen earns a reward, bestow it promptly, without grumbling or revising the parameters. If your teen's behavior triggers a consequence, be sure to see it through. As you enforce the minimum standards of respect for your home, keep this in mind: Deed is more important than creed. You can't require that teens feel respect for you, or even love; you can only require reasonably respectful behavior. They have to practice respect at home because they need *practice*.

Beware: Although the application of rules and consequences sounds bracingly simple on paper, it's always messy in real life. That's as it should be. Your child is new at being twelve or fifteen or seventeen, and you are new at being the parent of a teenager. Expect a learning curve. Let's imagine how Nancy might attempt to carry out a new family rule:

Nancy tells Theo he needs to take responsibility for his morning routine and asks him for suggestions. She explains that if she's going to drive him to school and be at her office on time, she needs to leave the house by eight o'clock, sharp. He says, "Okay, okay, I'll wake up by seven-thirty."

"What if you don't?" Nancy asks.

"If I oversleep, don't drive me. Just let me take the bus and be late."

This proposal irks Nancy on many counts, including the lack of breakfast and anticipation of multiple tardies, but she decides not to mention these. Instead, she says, "Okay, but for every tardy you have to stay in the next weekend night you planned on going out."

At first this plan does not work because neither party sticks to their agreement. The first morning, a Wednesday, Nancy sneaks by Theo's room at seven-forty and knocks. "Just wanted to see if you were getting started, sweetie." Theo groans, rolls over, and sleeps until eight. When he gets downstairs she hands him a quesadilla to eat in the car. They race to school just in time for the bell.

That evening after work, Nancy sits down with Theo to revisit and refine the rules. Again, she asks for his suggestions.

Theo says, "Not coming into my room means not talking to me outside the door. No communication. None. I will be down before eight. I need to sleep as late as possible. Once downstairs, I will not eat anything. The food truck comes by school during my ten a.m. free period, so I might eat something then. But nothing here. Nothing before I leave."

How obnoxious, Nancy thinks. *He's being so rude when I'm just trying to save him from himself . . . and from wasting money buying food at school when he can eat at home.* But again, she keeps her own counsel. She notices that Theo is suggesting that he will take full responsibility in the mornings if she will step out of his way.

The following morning brings a new twist. Theo oversleeps and Nancy leaves for work without him. Theo calls his friend Noah and hitches a ride. Same on Friday. Nancy is embarrassed that someone else is now entangled in their family problems but remains quiet. On Monday Theo gets up, throws on a T-shirt and flip-flops (even though the forecast is for cold and rain), and is downstairs at seven fifty-five. On Tuesday he oversleeps again; even his friend Noah has already left for school. He takes a taxi (paying with his own money), is late for school, and gets an "unexcused late arrival" on his record. When Nancy reminds him twice that he will have to stay in on Friday night, he makes a well-reasoned pitch:

"It's Noah's party, Mom! You can come, too, and hang out with his parents. You like them, and you should get out of the house more often. I'll stay in tomorrow night instead."

The pitch fails. "A tardy means you stay in the next time you planned on going out."

Theo accepts this consequence but requests that yet another rule be added to the newly developing list. "One more thing. If I have to stay in, you tell me *once*. You pick when. Otherwise every time you open your mouth I'm hearing about Friday night. It's worse than the punishment."

After Noah's missed party there are three more incidents of lateness. But then a steady change sets in. Theo is ready to leave for school on time every day. A few times, he actually talks to Nancy during the last five minutes of the drive. This pleasant conversational interlude is a product of his growing maturity and his positive feeling toward his calmer, less wimpy, less aggrieved mother.

MONEY IN THE BANK

Teens are more receptive to guidance if, with some regularity, they perceive their parents as allies. Invest in your teenager by showing goodwill toward them. Then, later, you can make a "withdrawal" on your store of benevolence when it is necessary to establish what are perceived as strict, old-fashioned, bizarre, or punitive rules about good manners.

I first heard this idea from Bob Ditter, a Boston-area psychologist who gives guidance to summer camp administrators and counselors. Ditter applies it to parents. After the kids arrive at camp he recommends that the counselors send a brief e-mail to each family telling them that the bus trip was happily uneventful and giving them one specific and personal detail about their child: "I'm already enjoying his sense of humor . . . so nice to have her bright smile in our group . . . he was so helpful to other kids as they unpacked . . . he proudly showed me his blue flippers." Ditter calls this small gesture "money in the bank." If the counselor has to call a parent about a behavior problem or rule violation later in the summer, there's already a foundation of familiarity and thoughtfulness in the relationship.

This approach will not create a perfectly functioning economy with teens, who are quite capable of forgetting everything nice you've ever done for them. Teens are unlikely to say, "Well, I'd *rather* go out with my friends tonight than visit Grandpa with you, but since you routinely treat me with great decency and respect . . . how can I say no?" Teens don't consciously measure the accumulation of goodwill, but they can feel it, and they frequently act on it—by agreeing to visit relatives or doing a load of laundry with less groaning than usual. Practicing kindness has additional advantages. For one, parents who spend a lot of time playing the heavy will find relief in being beneficent. Putting money in the bank of goodwill also teaches your teen that mature people practice kindness even when the recipient may not seem entirely deserving.

Look for opportunities to say yes to your teen's requests. Don't say it begrudgingly, or just because they've worn you down with their pestering. Express your agreement with enthusiasm, and make it expansive:

Sure.
Absolutely.
How great.
That sounds like fun.
I'll be glad to give you a ride if you need one.
I'd be happy to.
Certainly.
My pleasure.
Will you need some extra money for the evening?

Another way to invest in your teen is by honoring their food preferences, even when you find those preferences irritating. If your teen announces he will no longer eat anything that walks on four legs, buy brown rice and seitan for him, even if you have to throw some of it away when he switches back to hamburgers the next week. You've only spent a few dollars but have invested in respect. Or if you and your teen clash because you think he hangs out with a bad crowd, in the spirit of "keeping your enemies close" invite his favorite over to dinner. Maybe your teen will view him less favorably when he sees him afresh, through your eyes. Or maybe *you'll* discover that this "bad kid" is more a goofball than a hood. A change in perception, however, is not the point of the exercise; what matters most is your willingness to draw your teens' friends in and get to know them. Or try giving teens what they really want for their birthday. This probably felt natural and instinctive when they were small. But when they are testy and mercurial and unkind it's easy to take it personally and want to punish them, to become bitter or careless in your thoughtfulness. So all year long when they mention things they want to own, places they would like to go, experiences they would like to have, write them down. If the hard drive of your mind is overfull, write down where you put your list. And if your budget allows, flood them with a little undeserved generosity. If money is tight, pick up their favorite magazine or hair gel the next time you're at the drugstore.

THE HOLINESS OF MANNERS

You already know the practical reasons your teen needs to know respectful behavior and good manners. When your son's professor is thinking about which student to invite to join the research team, or he goes for his first job interview or is invited to spend the weekend with the parents of the young woman he wants to marry, you want him to be chosen. If he's rude, he is not going to find favor no matter how swell his GPA. Manners grease the wheels of society.

But respect for others goes beyond the quid pro quo of "I'll be nice to you if you'll be nice to me." It is a path to transcendence. The rabbis teach that although we will probably not come to know God as up close and personally as some of the biblical figures did, we can learn to know God through our actions—by embodying God, by acting in God's image. For example, God comforted Isaac when Abraham died, so if we act kindly to friends who are sad or sick with the sense that this is what God would do, the mere act of visiting takes on a distinctly spiritual color. It ties us to the tradition and to our people. It creates a sense of God's closeness.

This idea can be a source of deep solace for parents. Watching your teen pull away from you is painful. But when you guide your child with leadership that is respectful of their developmental phase and their individual spirit, you are traveling on a holy path.

CHAPTER 4

The Blessing of a B Minus:

The Real Lessons of Homework, Chores, and Jobs

When it came time for fall break during his freshman year at a top-tier college, my neighbor's son stuffed two months' worth of laundry—every piece of clothing he'd worn since arriving at school at the end of August—into three oversized suitcases, paid an excess baggage fee of one hundred fifty dollars to check them at the airport, and flew home to his parents' house.

"What were you thinking?" asked his astonished mother, as Josh deposited a mountain of smelly jeans, T-shirts, sweatshirts, and socks in the utility room and made his way to the kitchen.

"Mom," he said, opening the refrigerator, "how was I supposed to have time for laundry? I was studying . . . plus, I had all my work at the Hillel."

Josh is a good-hearted, generally responsible young man, not typically in the habit of taking advantage of his mother. But in high school, his parents had sheltered him from chores in exchange for his total devotion to schoolwork and extracurriculars. Now, in college, Josh was positive that this bargain was still in place—that academics and religious involvement gave him a free pass out of laundry duty. In Josh's mind, he was too gifted to sort his own socks.

It's tempting to protect our teens from the drudgery of chores and other work. They are up half the night writing papers about the role of the free market in medieval guilds; then they wake up at six a.m. for swim team practice; then they are at school for a long day. Plus, they are grouchy. Reminding them to clean the windows is asking for a fight when you are so, so tired of fighting.

But if you absolve your teen from routine responsibilities like laundry, you will teach him that there are two types of work: exalted and menial. In this distorted view, exalted work includes studying, practicing a sport, rehearsing a musical instrument, or tutoring children in a third-world country. It makes a teenager more accomplished, worldly . . . and attractive to college admissions departments. The second type of work—the kind that many teens believe is menial and beneath them—is the ordinary stuff: keeping track of all those homework assignments and turning them in on time; remembering to bring the necessary equipment to sports practices; automatically changing the toilet paper roll when it's down to a few sheets instead of leaving it for the next person; keeping track of the money left on their debit card, even during prom season; filling the family car with gas; and generally keeping the machinery of life oiled and humming. This kind of work is routine and sometimes tedious, but important. A large proportion of life is maintenance and repair. When parents let their teens believe they are too special to do ordinary work, they raise "handicapped royalty"—young people who study brilliantly and are full of conviction but don't know how clothes get clean or how to read a credit card bill.

These princes and princesses, despite their sparkling academic achievements, are in trouble when they enter the next phase of their lives. Keeping your clothes clean is important in and of itself, but it's also a metaphor for the self-reliance necessary to meet the other challenges of independence: managing a difficult roommate; gauging how much to drink and when and with whom; how much to eat; how much to sleep; how to budget your money; and how to plan both work and studying. Members of the handicapped royalty are overwhelmed by these details. They suffer from both loneliness (because they believe they are too special to cooperate with others) and anxiety (because they feel they are too fragile to cope with everyday life).

Our teens will be calmer and more responsible when they learn—and perform—ordinary tasks. But they won't bother trying if we, their parents, don't erase this false distinction between work that is worthy and work that is not.

GOD IS IN THE DETAILS

Rabbi Avi Weiss of the Hebrew Institute of Riverdale in New York tells this story:

A few years ago, a husband and wife appeared before Rabbi Gifter, Rosh Yeshiva of Tels, asking him to rule on a family dispute. The husband, a member of Rabbi Gifter's kollel (an all-day Torah learning program), felt that as one who studied Torah it was beneath his dignity to take out the garbage. His wife felt otherwise. Rabbi Gifter concluded that while the husband should in fact help his wife, he had no religious or legal obligation to remove the refuse.

The next morning, before the early services, the Rosh Yeshiva knocked at the door of the young couple. Startled, the man asked Rabbi Gifter in. No, responded Rabbi Gifter, I've come not to socialize but to take out your garbage. You may believe it's beneath your dignity, but it's not beneath mine.

Why would a rabbi take such pains to model the importance of mundane chores? Because, as I described in chapter 3, Judaism is a religion of deed over creed. Right actions, like helping your family by taking out the garbage, are more important than right belief. In another popular story, the Baal Shem Tov, the founder of the Chassidic movement, takes another rabbi's dirty coffee cups to the sink. When questioned about this activity, he responds that clearing dishes was a duty of the high priest on the Day of Atonement. In these and numerous other teaching tales, chores are a direct connection to God.

If we can pull away from our focus on the big, splashy, ego-gratifying activities of life, we can easily glimpse the holiness in workaday tasks. When we pull weeds from gardens and maintain our household files, we are creating order. When we set the table properly, with the napkin carefully creased down the middle, when we serve thoughtfully prepared food and then sweep the crumbs off the floor, we are elevating society. Modern theologian and Jungian Lawrence Corey points out that we can find holy sparks in "sharpening a pencil, cracking a nut, cleaning a cat box, [and] training a pet." In this view, God really *is* in the details. Taking out the garbage is as holy as finding a cure for cancer or jumping in a river and saving someone from drowning. It's as holy as making valedictorian.

IT'S NOT TOO LATE TO TEACH YOUR TEEN ORDINARY WORK

So you have a teenage child who apparently isn't aware of the cosmic impact of everyday chores, because he *never* takes out the garbage. Don't abandon hope. It's not too late for him to learn the value of ordinary work.

Start by not mentioning one word about the holiness of chores to your teen. If you share your precious pearls of spiritual wisdom, your teen will probably tune you out or write you off. All the more reason for you to shore up your inner conviction that ordinary work is good for your child. A change in your attitude—in your awareness and resolve—will lead to a change in your child's behavior, even if that child is stubborn and set in his ways. As parents, we cannot force our teens to love their boring, everyday duties. That's perfectly fine—as the rabbis tell us, actions are more important than beliefs. But as parents, we can use our own commitment, along with some practical knowledge of adolescent development, to guide our teens through three areas of cosmically important ordinary work: homework management, chores, and paid jobs.

DEFLATING THE DRAMA OF HOMEWORK

In elementary school, children become acquainted with studying and homework. In an ideal family situation, parents enforce rules about homework (such as "no television until your homework gets done") and the child completes the homework mostly without parental assistance. But in middle school, the amount of homework increases exponentially and so does the pressure to perform well on tests and quizzes. At this point, studying can take on the appearance of exalted work. When this happens, family roles become misaligned. The teen is expected to study, study, study while the parent acts as a cross between a sherpa, a concierge, and the secret police:

What do you mean, you have a Spanish test tomorrow? How long have you known about it? Why didn't you tell me? I'll bring you dinner on a tray while you hit the books.

Or:

I found your list of assignments for the week scrunched up at the bottom of your backpack. Are you or are you not aware that you have a history paper due on Friday? Look here and I'll show you the battle plan I've drawn up. Today I'll drive you to the library to do research, and tomorrow you'll show me the outline you've written. Wednesday you'll draft the paper, and let's save Thursday so I can look it over for you.

Step back. Put down your tray and walk away from the schedule. By viewing academics so reverently and believing that your child requires your high-powered intervention, you are missing the point. The purpose of homework is not to bring glory to the family in the form of perfect grades. It is an ordinary chore. A chore that will teach your child less about the quadratic equation or the Maginot Line than about the cognitive abilities called executive functions: planning, prioritizing, delay of gratification, and tolerance of frustration. Executive functions may not sound glamorous, but without them, people are unable to set goals and achieve them.

This brings me to Shawn (not a real boy, but a composite of several I've known; his story will give you the flavor of a typical teenaged thought process) and his eighth-grade science paper—the paper his teacher wants him to research, write, revise, and proofread on his own. The one his parents don't believe it is possible for him to satisfactorily complete without their active oversight. But let's look at what happens when his parents *don't* treat him like handicapped royalty, when they let him follow the predictable learning curve of inspiration, resistance, feedback, and confidence.

Inspiration

I think there's a mini Snickers bar in the bottom of my backpack. Hmm, what's this paper sticking to it? Oh, it's the assignment Ms. Cross handed out. Let's see when . . . two weeks ago. Whoa, it's due on Wednesday! That gives me only today and tomorrow to finish it. "Contrast and compare the geocentric and heliocentric models of the solar system." Okay, I'm cool. I know astronomy. The big bang, black holes, tarantula nebula. I used to love this stuff. When I was in fourth grade I was always drawing pictures of comets crashing into the earth. I bet I drew hundreds. Maybe I could do illustrations for the cover of my paper. Sweet.

Having recalled his former love of flaming space debris, Shawn is abuzz with the first jolt of creative inspiration. Inspiration is personal; you cannot supply it for your teen. If Shawn's parents had been standing in the room with him ("Okay, Shawn, let's get started. What do you want to write about? How about asteroids? You used to like them so much, remember?"), they might easily have blocked his enthusiastic identification with the topic.

Resistance

Inspiration is inevitably followed by resistance, which itself can take creative forms: boredom, a sense of defeat, self-doubt, resentment, being overwhelmed, confused, hungry, thirsty, tired, lonely, itchy, urgently in need of learning a new guitar chord. Let's pay a visit to more of Shawn's thought process:

What's this? "No Web resources permitted for this paper." I'll just take a peek at Wikipedia anyway. Can't hurt. Here's a book listed at the bottom of the entry on the geocentric model: Arthur Koestler, The Sleepwalkers: A History of Man's Changing Vision of the Universe, 1959. *Man, that sounds like a classic. I'm sure it's in the school library. Right. So I don't have to actually go there, do I? What else? "Please take care to use proper punctuation and to write all footnotes in MLS style." Oh. I'm getting sleepy. Very sleepy.*

Okay, now I've written a page from the notes I took in class. Maybe I should spell-check and fix all the errors. Or print it out and read it on paper. Why is the printer blinking instead of printing? Maybe it will start working if I go downstairs and get something to drink. Or take a short TV break. What's on? Oh my God. I can't believe it. Deep Impact. *That's amazing. I practically have to watch it because it's about an asteroid. I can finish the paper tomorrow. I'll just stay up really late. I'll have more energy by then. Or maybe Ms. Cross will talk about the paper in class tomorrow and she'll explain a lot. That will make it easier. Yeah, I'm done for today.*

This natural resistance is why talent is never a sufficient condition for art. One of the deepest benefits of doing homework is to learn how to overcome resistance, to keep the engine chugging uphill after the initial wave of inspiration or interest or excitement has passed. And to learn to do this on your own.

Feedback

If you, the parent, allow Shawn to make his own mistakes, life will teach its lessons. These are the lessons Shawn discovers in the trenches in between the craving for a candy bar and the handing in, a day late, of a hastily completed paper, with inappropriate footnotes (Koestler's book was not among the school library holdings), for which he receives a disappointing grade of B minus (a mark that, in this era of grade inflation and high anxiety, is considered unacceptable by many parents).

This is what psychologists call a natural consequence. When you resist acting as your teen's tutor or personal assistant, the real world steps in to help. From this perspective, bad outcomes are good. The sting of points off for lateness, or a lower grade for a rushed, sloppy, or skimpy job, is priceless. Your child is given the automatic feedback mechanism of effort in relation to outcome.

Interference with this natural feedback loop is one of the reasons teachers are frustrated by parental management of homework. When a parent nervously overcontrols a teen's homework schedule, or when a parent reads and corrects the homework, the student doesn't have the opportunity to learn the nuanced relationship between his effort and his outcomes. ("Oh, if I watch a movie instead of writing the paper, the paper doesn't turn out so well.") The teacher, too, is deprived of the information she needs to tailor the curriculum to the student's learning needs by finding out where students individually and collectively need help. ("Looks like I need to devote class time to the art of writing opening paragraphs.")

If you step in when your teenager first runs into resistance, you send unintended messages:

- *The work is unbearable* (no, it isn't, it's just unfamiliar, he doesn't have a track record of completed science papers yet)
- *It's too much for him* (no, it isn't, he is sufficiently capable and intelligent)
- *It is so terribly important for him to do well on every single assignment—after all, he's just one year away from high school and the permanent transcript—that we can't take any chances* (no, it's just one paper out of many)

We unwittingly send the message that our children are not capable when we offer help with manageable but often uncomfortable or irksome tasks.

Does this mean you have to just sit back and watch them fail? Sometimes. But while you should not manage their homework for them, you are welcome to help teens stop procrastinating. Some see homework as boring torture, and they make it much worse by dragging it out. You can teach them the wisdom of the old saying "The only way out is through." Others put off their homework because they have difficulty getting started or because they are overwhelmed by the size of a task. By active listening you can support, your child without swallowing him up; rather than intruding or solving problems, you can offer respectful guidance. If he's having trouble getting the paper started, you can ask about obstacles he's facing:

"I can see you're frustrated about the way your work piles up on Thursday nights. What do you think might help?"

"Well, they did give us these weekly homework planners at the beginning of the school year. But only Danielle Greenberg uses them, and you know what she's like. . . . I guess I could try writing my assignments in it. If I remember."

Or:

"You look overwhelmed. What's on your mind?"

"Whenever I sit down to work, I feel like I don't even know where to start."

"Yeah, I always feel like that when I have to write presentations. Getting started is the hardest part for me, too. Do you ever talk about that in class?"

"Mrs. Michaels says that everyone has trouble writing the first paragraph. She said some people like to write the body of the essay first and then write the opening."

"Sounds like a good idea."

You can also help your teen help himself with homework by removing stumbling blocks. For a teenager, technology is a major stumbling block on the way to concentrated effort. A computer has everything an easily distracted young person longs for: music, chats, Facebook, mail, and side trips to YouTube. Although every self-respecting teen claims to be a master of multitasking, the steady blip, blip, blip of instant messages is far more alluring than choosing a topic sentence for an English essay. If your teen is struggling with homework completion, remember that it's her ordinary work. You may need to require her to place her cell phone outside her door and disable and password protect the wireless connection to her laptop until milestones in her work are met. Old-fashioned person-to-person socializing is a common stumbling block, too. When work piles up, allow your teen to go out with her friends . . . *after* her work is finished.

Confidence

Two months later. Shawn works on Earth Science paper number four. Here's a portrait of a boy who is not handicapped royalty. It can happen at your house:

(Checking his weekly planner.) *Paper coming up soon. I should ask Mom tonight if she can pick me up late after school on Tuesday so I can spend some time in the library doing research and working on the bibliography, then I'll write the paper on Wednesday. I'll need to borrow the style manual back from Sam so I'll have it at home. I'll do the final draft on Thursday after I study for the math test . . . this should work out just fine.*

CHORES: THE CURRICULUM OF LIFE

As time-consuming as homework is, don't let it prevent you from assigning chores to your teen. Conquering your ambivalence about this will be a challenge. Yes, your teen has to do a lot of studying, rehearsing, and practicing. Certainly, your teen deserves a social life. And yes, we're all busy, and often it's easier to do everything yourself than to wait for a slow-paced, sloppy, preoccupied teen to do it. But chores are the curriculum of life. And the tuition is free!

Tasks such as learning to do the laundry, cleaning out the basement, and taking care of pets are a more robust lesson in competence than any SAT prep course. In my experience, chores lead to better school performance because they teach teens how to organize their time and their actions. Chores form a foundation for the rest of life as well. Young adults with household skills know how to carry their own weight. They help clean up after a college kegger; they clear dishes while visiting a girlfriend's family; they contribute to making a shared dorm room or house a pleasant living environment. They're conscious of ways to help without being told or asked. They aren't crippled by the depressing belief that only the less talented or unexceptional perform the necessary chores of daily life. And because of their skills and willingness to pitch in, they're considered kind, respectful, and appealing.

If your teen doesn't already have a set of chores to do, write out a list of jobs that need to be done around the house on a weekly, monthly, and seasonal basis. Then hold a family meeting to divvy them up. Although your family is not a democracy, your teen's "buy in" will be greater if he has some say in which chores will be his responsibility. Let him pick a few he actually enjoys . . . or finds the least repellent. One of my daughters enjoys using the pressure washer on the patio, while the other one likes to sort and discard kitchen items and clothes. If nothing appeals to your teen, assign chores according to his talents and temperament. If your teen is an organized shopper, give him a grocery list and drop him off at the supermarket. If he has lots of restless energy and loves heights, have him clean the downspouts. Remember that the point of chores is to lighten the load on the family and teach your teen, not torment him. Though chores can be consequences for bad behavior, don't use them as punishment for aspects of his personality you find unappealing. ("You can't figure out how to organize your desk? Well, congratulations, mister, you'll organize the entire garage! *That'll* teach you!") Next *you* have to follow through. Making sure your teen does chores is a dull but essential responsibility of your own.

Dishwasher Loading Technique as Crystal Ball

I know, it's easy for me to wax on about raising your teen's chore consciousness when I don't live with him. Your son may volunteer for dishwasher duty, but he loads it in a sloppy fashion: wineglasses wedged next to pots, a salad bowl (so easy to wash in the sink) on the bottom rack taking up space that could hold half a dozen plates, tomato sauce glazing the silverware so the whole interior reeks when you open the door to add the cereal bowls you find scattered about the family room.

How do you react? You might take the disappointment personally: *If he really loved me, if he appreciated the trouble I take to make his meals, he would do a better job.* Or you might move from the specific, particular act of careless dishwasher loading to a general judgment of character: *He's a careless person . . . probably because of my lousy parenting. Or my in-laws' bad genes.* An angry reaction to teen disorderliness can also be a symptom of other troubles weighing on your mind. Like my patient who checked and rechecked that the door was locked rather than addressing her anger at her spouse, parents sometimes shrink their bigger problems (marriage, finances) down to a worm's-eye view (a focus on a son's improper loading technique). Taking the worm's-eye view makes life's problems feel tidy, more manageable, but only for a while. That's because a healthy teen will not only reject your misplaced outrage, he'll hand it back to you with a little extra of his own:

Mom: *Jason, come down right now and look at this. You're the one who's always talking about being eco-conscious. Do you know how much water it wastes when you don't put things in properly?*

Jason: *I don't know why I try. I can't do anything right. You always pick on me about the smallest things. What if I were tagging like my friend Max? Then you wouldn't be complaining about how I load the dishwasher. You would just be glad I wasn't arrested for having a trunk full of spray paint cans and weed.*

Don't invest your teen's sloppiness and bad attitude with too much meaning. It'll just make you unhappy. Instead, comfort yourself with knowledge about adolescent development. Teens are dopamine machines; their brains are wired to seek out novelty and excitement. It's hard for them to slow down and focus on boring activities like loading the dishwasher. Another reason they appear careless is that their prefrontal cortex is not fully developed, so tasks such as categorizing dishes by size and most appropriate washing method can be challenging for them. And then there's the challenge of physical growth. You know how pregnant women are always spilling stuff down the front of their shirts because they aren't accustomed to their changing size? A teen is in a similar predicament. Teenagers' hands and feet are still growing; it's easy for them to misjudge the space between racks and break a plate. So while they may display stunning dexterity while texting and playing Rock Band, the delicate hand-eye coordination required by the dishwasher may be beyond their current level of physical grace. It's not about you, or about how poorly you've raised them. They just need time and practice. Insist on chores but don't be nitpicky. Try on a new philosophy: If the dishes get clean and don't break, your son did what you asked him to do.

When you give your teenager a job to do, let him know ahead of time what your standards are: "Okay, so you'll scrape the dishes and load them into the dishwasher each night. You'll do this after dinner and before you have any computer time. Any questions?" Then let him, as much as is reasonable, decide how to get it done. Don't insist that he do it precisely the way you would. He is learning, and you're an expert. He has his rhythm; honor it, even though yours is probably speedier and more efficient. It's fine if he wants to play music, or pause to play with the dog. If he wants your company, consider appreciating the opportunity to spend time together rather than seeing it as a ploy to slack off.

Surrender to the Messy Bedroom

The kitchen, family room, shared bathrooms, and hallways are common areas of the house. There, your children should observe your family's standard of neatness. Yes, you understand that they've had a taxing day, but they are still required to pick up their backpacks and coats from the floor. Yes, they need to feed the dog before they do anything else. But a teen's bedroom, well, it's a common battleground, and in this case I suggest a partial surrender. Like rudeness, sleeping until noon, or eating two suppers in a single night, messiness is endemic to being a teenager. The whole process of growing up is messy, so the messy room is an accurate representation of what's going on inside. Teenagers don't have a new self yet, and they are convinced that to form an identity they need to keep all the apparatus from their old self—the stuffed animals, magic tricks, Bratz dolls, gaming DVDs, and every baseball hat, T-shirt, barrette, pen, bottle of nail polish, or tube of lip gloss they have ever owned.

And all this apparatus of theirs is emotionally loaded. Time is very rich and full to teenagers; every minute is weighted with significance. They don't want to throw away a gum wrapper because it's infused with the memory of when they got it, what the gum tasted like, who they were with, and whether it was a sad or happy occasion. Teens act cynical but are tremendously sentimental, and their room is the vortex of all that feeling.

If your teen consistently cannot find things he needs, such as schoolwork, money, car keys, or important papers, or if he is hoarding old food or dirty dishes, it's time for him to clean up. Other than that, the room is not your business. Two mothers in my parenting class had the right idea. One said she didn't mind her son's messiness because the new carpeting in his room was getting so little wear she knew it would last a long, long time. Another said that her only neatness requirement was that her daughter make an earthquake evacuation path from the desk and bed to the door.

When to Hit the Reset Button

You have made your list of chores, let your teen take his pick, issued your minimum standards, and then backed off . . . and your house is still a disaster. The dishes don't get loaded, or they don't get clean. The mess in his bedroom spills out not just into the hallway but also the living room and porch. Rather than carping, change your tactics.

First, make sure that you're modeling a reasonably reverent attitude toward chores. Do you expect your child to hang up all her clothes neatly, but feel it's perfectly reasonable for *you* or your spouse to leave dirty socks on the floor? If so, you're creating a double standard. Do you leave all the cleaning to a housekeeper because you work so very hard? If so, you are teaching your child the lesson that busy people don't have to clean up after themselves. Do you perform your chores obsessively but complain all the while? Or resentfully vacuum under your child's feet while he watches his favorite TV show? You're teaching your child that chores are a dreary substitute for life, not a practical way to enhance it. Clean up your own attitude, and you may see a change in your teen's.

If changing your attitude doesn't solve the problem, talk to your teen directly about it. Try saying something like, "Our system for chores isn't working. I'm nagging you all the time, and you're angry." Or, "When I come home in the evening I can't be sure that the dogs have been fed. When you feed them only sometimes but not all the time, it's almost worse than not at all. I don't want to have to worry about this anymore." Put your heads together, come up with some new approaches, and agree to try again.

Another approach is to rethink your teen's set of chores. Go back to your list of household chores and reassess. If your teen initially volunteered to load the dishwasher but has shown himself to be too klutzy or too distractible to do it well, suggest that he might like to wash your car instead. One of the definitions of insanity is doing the same things over and over and expecting a different outcome. If we are too rigid about our requirements, if we fuss too much over the need for a teen to perform one specific chore, we are missing the point of ordinary work. We're not giving teens the opportunity to perform these homely, holy tasks with confidence and pride.

Redefine Privileges

However, when teens are chronically noncompliant with chores, you need to issue consequences. Remember the principle that you are

required to provide your teen with appropriate clothes, good schooling, shelter, and nourishing food. Anything else is a privilege that can be
taken away when house rules are violated.

When you issue consequences, expect resistance in the form of
excuses:

*I am going to do the dishes, but I was going to let the burned stuff in the pan
soak for a while.*

Or feigned apathy:

Go ahead, take the computer out of my room. I don't care.

Or surgically precise attacks on your self-esteem:

*You're just acting this way because you gave up your career and now your
only source of pride is a freakishly clean house.*

Don't take the bait. Don't escalate the argument or show how horri-
bly hurt and wounded you are, because if your teen discovers a rhetorical weapon that distracts you from the business at hand, you can bet he
will use it again and again and again. Remain calm. By ignoring these
comments, you'll let him know they don't work. Say, "Nevertheless,
you didn't do the dishes and now you lose computer privileges for the
night."

Taking a privilege away from your teen is hard, I know. He's surly
enough as it is. But if your teen doesn't do chores, if you take on all the
responsibility for dishes and cleaning and yard work, your child won't
learn self-reliance, and you will get angry and resentful. This is not a
dignified stance for a parent. And your house won't look nice! Your
house—the container of the family—is a holy place. It should be a reasonably civilized and orderly environment. (You don't need to mention
any of this to your teen; just recite it to yourself when you need the
courage to enforce chores.)

I'm not making any promises, but the risk you take in getting your
touchy, distant teen to do chores can result in an unexpected emotional payoff. That's because doing chores *with* teens can be the most
fun you have together. Organizing the closet or weeding the yard
together is conducive to casual conversation, the kind you may not
have had in a while. Sometimes—*sometimes*—that conversation will
turn deep, and in a much more natural way than if you enter your
teen's room, sit on the edge of the bed, and demand a serious heart-
to-heart.

WHY A PAID JOB IS BETTER THAN
AN EXOTIC VOLUNTEER EXPERIENCE

In addition to homework and chores, I want your child to have a paid job—a *real,* ordinary job. College admissions officers do, too.

One evening I was part of a panel discussion with a group of college admissions officers from elite private colleges. The subject of "trends in selection criteria" came up, and one of the panelists mentioned her preference for candidates who have held down a job. The others nodded in agreement.

A mother in the audience raised her hand and waved it back and forth with great vigor: "My daughter has been to a program . . . in"—and here she paused dramatically, her voice lowered to an almost whispery tremble—"Africa." She went on: "The students *volunteered* in the *community.* They helped local children do crafts, taught them some *English words,* and helped build a shed to store gardening equipment behind the school."

A panelist responded, "We laugh at Africa."

Obviously, he did not mean that college admissions officers laugh at those in need. They laugh at parents' mistaken belief that popular "summer volunteer experience" programs look impressive on a college application. Why aren't colleges awed by kids who lay pipes in Kenya? For the same reason I'm not: When teenagers participate in a community service program paid for by their parents, whether in Africa or closer to home, they are not working for money. The adults who run the program are. Like cruise ship entertainment directors, these adults want repeat business with your other children or good word of mouth in the school or temple or church. They want you to say to all your friends:

Chloe had the best time! There were screens on the windows, not too many mosquitoes—thank God there's no malaria in that part of the country. She didn't even get a bad sunburn.

There are similar problems with the kind of "internships" in which parents rig up a summer position at their company for their child or their friend's child. The responsibilities are minimal and often manufactured, with little contribution to the business. For kids at these internships, nothing's on the line. Their actions don't affect the business; they can't even get fired except for gross misconduct. They spend most of their time bugging the grown-ups to give them some work to do, or trying to look busy. College admissions officers know this, which is why on page four of the Common Application, you will see a section that reads:

> Work Experience:
> Please list **paid** jobs you have held during the past three years (including summer employment).

Note that the word "paid" is in bold.

A paid job is one of the best ways to teach teens respect, self-discipline, maturity, and integrity—four traits on which your child's teachers will rate her when they fill out the Common Application's teacher recommendation form. A paid job is the exact opposite of supervised transcript fodder like volunteer experiences and internships. In a paid job, the teen is often working for adults, so she has to cater *to them*. The adult pays the teen to show up on time, do what is asked of her and more, dress appropriately, be respectful, keep her work area neat, avoid procrastination, tolerate criticism (even unfair criticism), and learn to be part of a hierarchy that consists of many different and possibly irritating personalities. When a problem arises on the job—the child she's baby-sitting starts to vomit, or the popcorn popper spews butter-flavored oil all over the concession stand where she works solo, or a customer complains that the teen has rung up the wrong price of her milk—the young employee has to decide how to solve it. Clean up the mess, locate a wrench, cheerfully correct the mistake.

Baskin Robbins University

Your teen could find an undemanding job for the summer—say, parking luxury cars at a country club for generous tips. If practical, discourage this kind of easy-money work. The less glamorous your child's job, the better.

When she was in high school, my friend Laurie Goodman spent a summer working in a bicycle factory. Her job was to pick up kickstands (covered in grease to prevent rust) and put them into a plastic bag. For eight hours a day. The foreman would walk down the line, barking at the employees to work faster. She and a friend distracted themselves from the repetition and indignity by singing songs from Broadway musicals to each other. Almost literally, they learned to whistle while they worked.

This was a lesson in itself, but there was more. The two girls realized they could pull off this slight, face-saving insouciance because it was only a summer job, whereas their coworkers, who depended on their jobs and couldn't risk annoying the foreman, stayed silent.

Working at a nonfancy job meets the latest "trends in selection criteria" for college admissions, but it also teaches the cosmic lesson of empathy, of walking in the shoes of people who work very, very hard for low wages. It teaches you that service is not servility and that any job can be done with dignity. It motivates you to work hard in school when you see how easily low-wage/low-skill jobs become boring or repetitive. Whereas easy-money jobs teach you that money and life are always just that: easy.

Instead of sending your teen to Africa, consider enrolling her for a summer session at Baskin Robbins University. Your child will scoop servings of hard, gummy ice cream out of a vat. She'll be cold. She might get a repetitive stress injury of the wrist. She might grow bored with asking, "Cup or cone? Sugar or plain? Would you like a lid on that?" She'll be paid minimum wage, but the experience will be worth pure gold.

Yes, But . . .

Your teen may offer several passionately argued objections to getting a job:

Mom, I would NEVER wear that stupid uniform where my friends can see me.

After they take the taxes out I earn exactly . . . nothing!

The Bergmans are asking me to baby-sit EVERY Saturday night. That's like my whole weekend. That's my only chance to hang out with my friends.

But if you are committed to the practical and spiritual value of paid work, you can easily quiet these protests. How? With the magical tool of requiring teens to earn their own spending money. When your teen's acquisition of an iPhone depends on her weekly paycheck, you will be amazed at her willingness to don a movie theater uniform: shiny, oversized bellhop-style jacket, topped off with a bellhop-style hat.

Yes, your teen's objections can be overcome. But what about your objections? Your misgivings about the time a job takes, about its safety, about availability? Let's take a look.

Objection: The jobs I had as a teen—delivering newspapers, mowing lawns—are harder to come by now.

Some traditional teen jobs, especially jobs for boys, are now the province of low-wage adult workers. But if you keep your eyes open, you'll find opportunities for teens of both sexes. A few of these are:

Usher at a movie theater
Barista
Server or busboy at a restaurant
Camp counselor
Fast-food worker
Activities coordinator at a family resort
Assistant in a kids' birthday-party facility (The Bounce Zone, Chuck E. Cheese)
Lifeguard
Amusement park/theme park worker
Tutor for younger kids—for schoolwork, art, or a musical instrument
Coach or referee for children's sports teams
Retail clerk
Bagger in a grocery store
Baby-sitter (teen boys who can handle rowdy, sportive younger boys can carve out a lucrative niche for themselves)

Objection: Between extracurriculars and homework, there's no time for an afterschool job.

This may be true. You may decide to require your teens to work full-time during the summer but allow them to spend the school year focused on studies and activities.

But in my experience, teens are energized by paid work. Their real-world responsibilities are exciting to them, and the work habits they learn on the job translate into greater efficiency with homework, music lessons, and other tasks. For these reasons, I always expected my daughters to work year-round. Summer was the season for more traditional jobs: camp counselor and retail clerk. During the school year, these jobs either vanished or came with minimum-hour requirements that were too high to maintain. (For most students, more than fifteen hours of work per week is likely to affect school performance or sleep.) Instead, Emma and Susanna came up with jobs that were more entrepreneurial and far less time-consuming. Emma drove a school carpool, taking other students to school each day in exchange for a vigorously negotiated fee. No, it didn't require her to answer to adults, but it did require her to take initiative, to collect and handle money, *and* to wake up twenty minutes early on every single weekday morning of the school year—a big commitment for a sleepy teenager. Susanna designed, made, and sold her own jewelry to local stores. Both babysat. One of their friends produced video montages to be shown at birthday parties and anniversaries; another hired himself out as a disc jockey on the weekend; others tutored younger kids.

Objection: Lifeguarding was okay when we were young, but now, with the ozone layer so thin, it's too dangerous.

I can't let her walk through the mall parking lot to her car at night.

I can't let her work in a fast-food restaurant! She could get shot!

These worries remind me of the parents of younger children who are too afraid to let their kids walk out the front door to visit a friend three houses away. Danger is the excuse we give for forbidding a certain activity, but our real fear is losing control over our children's lives. We especially fear handing our children over to people we don't know. Since birth, our kids' playgroups, doctors, schools, synagogues, playmates, tutors, and coaches have been carefully handpicked. We screen out any potential bad influences. Our kids may be happy and relaxed in the bubble we've created, but they are also oddly isolated. Teens make their bubbles even smaller. High school lunchrooms are notoriously segregated according to the local tribes: preppy kids, drama kids, skateboarders, Goth kids, indie kids, cheerleading squad.

A job is integrating. Relationships there are less competitive than at school, and at work your teen may mix it up with teens who sit on the other side of the lunchroom, far, far from her usual table. She may meet adults who are earthier, more straightforward, more authentic, or even crazier than the adults at home. For our hothouse flowers, contact with new people is healthy and invigorating.

Objection: My teen feels too much pressure and responsibility as it is. Aren't you the person who's always suggesting that we ease up on our kids?

The lives of teens are full of manufactured responsibilities: Get good grades, be captain of this, star of that. They feel as if their whole future is at stake, every moment, when of course it isn't.

A job offers real-life responsibility. A teen goes from the constructed responsibility of "Get an A in trigonometry" to "You are responsible for the safety of swimmers at our wave park," or "You are responsible for taking care of three young children for an evening," or "You must make sure the cash drawer comes out even at the end of your shift." If a teen is reliable and dependable, he earns even more responsibility. The moment a teenager is trusted with "key" responsibilities—literally, being given a key to the bead store or pretzel kiosk and allowed to open it in the morning—is a moment of earned pride.

When a teen's skills don't easily fit into the society-approved categories of achievement—academics, athletics, music, drama, student government—work can be an alternative avenue to confidence. I'm reminded of Natalie, a girl I saw when she was fifteen and going through a rough patch. Natalie had few friends because of her prickly nature; she fought with her parents; and she was often benched for poor sportsmanship on her basketball team. She found a haven when she began to work for an animal rescue group she discovered online, helping to match dogs with families who would like to adopt them. In this position of leadership, Natalie was mature beyond her years. At work, kids like Natalie, freed by the employer's lack of concern for their SAT scores, can discover surprising talents: organizing, selling, managing, solving problems, and taking initiative. Not coincidentally, these are the skills most highly prized by future employers, who may hire based on a graduate's résumé but who promote based on practical skills.

DAILY WORK IS A GIFT

When children are young it is necessary to do so much for them. No matter how tired you are, no matter how many times you have to change the sheets in one night, no matter how colicky the baby, you aim to be dutiful and kind. After years and years of practice, the habit of protecting, fixing, patching, and repairing becomes a reflex. It's hard to know when and how to stop or slow down. But if you do not reverse some of these impulses as your child grows, if you protect your child from learning the basic skills of life, he will not have the chance to become self-sufficient. Overprotecting your child in this way is like hand-feeding a maturing bird; it will be well nourished but unable to forage for food on its own. But if you teach your child that everyday work is a gift, you encourage skills that will allow him to develop his holy potential—first as a child and student, and eventually as a parent and contributing member of the community.

CHAPTER 5

The Blessing of a Lost Sweater:

Managing Your Teen's Materialism, Entitlement, and Carelessness

Now that sixteen-year-old Asher has taken an online tutorial on how to play the electric guitar and his friend Lucas has taught him three chords, he considers himself a serious student of the instrument. He practices, intermittently, late at night, and the neighbors are complaining. Asher is undaunted and lobbies his parents for a new guitar to replace the serviceable one handed down from his brother:

Robbie's old Yamaha sounds like crap. If you would just come with me to Guitar Center, you could hear how much better the Fender sounds. And the Silvermans are right about the noise. We have to soundproof the garage. You can just move some of the boxes from the garage to the back of your closet and take the rest of the stuff down to the basement.

"We call him the Sun King," Asher's parents say about their teenager. "How did we raise a child who believes the earth revolves around him? And how can we teach him not to treat us like his personal housekeeping service and ATM?"

Reasonable questions. Although Asher's parents need to work on guiding him out of his self-absorption, they don't need to panic. An extravagant sense of entitlement is normal for teenagers, a necessary way station on the path to adulthood.

YOUR NORMAL NARCISSIST

Here are the characteristics listed in the American Psychiatric Association's definition of narcissistic personality disorder:

1 Has a grandiose sense of self-importance
2 Is preoccupied with fantasies of unlimited success, power, brilliance, beauty, or ideal love
3 Believes that he or she is "special" and unique and can only be understood by other special people
4 Requires excessive admiration
5 Has a strong sense of entitlement
6 Takes advantage of others to achieve his or her own ends
7 Lacks empathy
8 Is often envious or believes others are envious of him or her
9 Arrogant attitude or bearing

Sound like anyone you know? Someone living under your own roof, perhaps? Thoughts, feelings, and actions that are pathological at one stage of life are normal at another. Just as ADHD-like behavior is the norm for many young boys and preoccupation with the past is typical for the elderly, narcissistic behavior is normal for most teenagers. One of the most irritating qualities of this self-centeredness is their conviction that they are entitled to a broad array of goods and services, even at the expense of others. Like Asher, most teens believe that in order to learn, grow, and thrive, their contentment must be assured at all costs.

From a developmental perspective, this unrelenting self-centeredness is useful for teens, a way for them to exercise influence in a world run by adults. Remember when your teen was a helpless infant? Your baby's cry was so piercing and unpleasant that you were compelled to use every bit of intelligence, sensitivity, and endurance you possessed to figure out how to relieve the distress. (*Is he actually hungry again? Could he be cold in this warm room? Is the diaper tape pinching his skin?*)

Adolescents deploy the same strategy. They are not helpless, but they don't have command of adult power, either. Younger teens can't drive or vote or make major purchases, so instead they pester you past all reason. They deliver their demands with hormonally driven urgency. They are so miserable about your refusal to drive them to Katie's house right away, or passionately in need of a new hoodie, or confident that their history project will be a smash if you just stay up late and help them, that you may relent, just to have some peace.

But your child's job is to make presumptuous demands, to communicate a great sense of desperation, and your job is not to get your knickers in a twist. One of the joys of parenting is providing your children with the little extras—gifts and services that aren't strictly necessary but that bring them pleasure and help them feel safer and more protected in their world of constant transition. But if you consistently jump up and start running whenever your teen issues a demand, you'll end up bitter and angry, and your child will develop what psychologist Jerome Kagan calls "oversatiation of desire," a condition created by having too many needs met by others. An oversatiated child behaves like a baby or a bully, but her attitude actually develops out of a sense of impotence. Children who have been pampered come to feel that they must rely on others to satisfy and entertain them. They lack faith in their own ability to fix their problems. How does a compassionate parent accept their teenager's developmental narcissism while encouraging their child to decenter, to rely on internal strengths rather than material indulgence? The Jewish concept of the *yetzer hara* (evil inclination) provides a useful guide to parents who are perplexed by their teen's greediness.

THE *YETZER HARA*

Judaism commands contentment. Each year at Rosh Hashanah we are reminded, "Let us not be consumed by desire for what we lack or grow unmindful of the blessings we already have." Sound advice. But how can parents teach gratitude to teenagers? How to respond to teens who want a new camera when they left the last one on the bus? Or who feel that you are obligated to pick up the jersey they left at a friend's house and drop it off at the field for them before practice begins?

In *The Blessing of a Skinned Knee,* I explained Judaism's unusual perspective on human nature. The ancient rabbis believed that each of us harbors an aggressive impulse called the *yetzer hara.* Although the *yetzer hara* can lead to greedy selfishness and violence, it is also a source of animating energy. The rabbis respected the *yetzer hara* so deeply that they dubbed it *tov meod* (very good).

A story in the Talmud illustrates the cosmic power of the *yetzer hara.* The men of the Great Assembly, wishing to eliminate all the pain created by the *yetzer hara,* captured it and locked it up. The *yetzer hara* called out from its prison: "If you kill me the world will go down!" The men ignored this grandiose and improbable warning, but soon they discovered the grim truth in it. Searching the land for a newly laid egg during the *yetzer's* exile, they could not find a single one. In Hebrew the word *"yetzer"* (impulse) has the same root as the word *"yetzira,"* which means "creation." Without the evil inclination there is no possibility of new life. Nor can there be passion or enthusiasm, ambition, creativity, or imagination—and, consequently, the rabbis explain, there can be no marriages, no children conceived, no businesses or bustling cities.

When teens ask for more clothes, more equipment, more "just this once" favors, you can get angry at their selfishness . . . or you can pause, step back, and marvel at the presence of the energetic, passionate *yetzer hara*. Seen through this lens, their lusty acquisitiveness, even for things that are not to your taste, is a lust for life itself. For busy adults, shopping frequently falls into one of two categories: dull chore or retail therapy. And certainly some teens use shopping as a quick lift, too, a distraction from their troubles. But for most of them, shopping is an exuberant form of self-expression. Watch a cluster of teens at a vintage clothing store, and you'll notice how much energy they bring to the hunt. They love to dig through the sale tables, the ones with other people's castoffs piled in big heaps. To parents it may look like a pile of dirty laundry; to them it's a chance to pan for gold. They say, "Ohmygod! Ohmygod! Look at this jacket! Look, it's one hundred percent wool." Even the "two for one" items at the teen jewelry emporium at the mall—when the "one" comprises five pairs of thin metal earrings on a little card—are treated like buried treasure. They buy things—extremely baggy or extremely tight pants—that are fantastical, silly, or sexy to help them freely try on new identities. At the same time, they shop to fit in with their current group. The styles of jeans, shoes, and even ponytail holders must broadcast solidarity with their friends. And they shop to look forward to the future, to the fun they will have wearing their purchases to the semiformal, the concert, the party, or the game. This is the vibrancy, the life force, of the materialistic *yetzer hara*.

The downside of the teen's *yetzer* is that it is shallow, capricious, and careless with the very thing it coveted so much the day before—not to mention heedless of the family budget. Of course you don't want to encourage your teen's *yetzer hara* to run wild. That's just as counterproductive as confining it to a cage. Judaism teaches that we live best when we balance the energy of the *yetzer hara* with the virtue of self-control. We are not meant to live like animals, satisfying our every urge. Nor should we strive to imitate the angels, who are never tempted by earthly delights. We have been endowed at birth with free will, which allows us to choose which desires we will satiate and which ones we will sublimate. This power allows us to delay gratification in order to reach a goal; to put the needs of others ahead of our own; and to heighten our pleasure in what we already have.

Striking the proper balance of energy and restraint is a lifelong challenge, but it is particularly difficult in the adolescent years, when the *yetzer hara* is a bold presence. How can parents honor the *yetzer hara's* zesty spirit while guiding their teens toward greater self-control and gratitude? You can't expect teens not to lust after a seventh pair of skinny jeans, but you can teach them the satisfaction of saving for what they really want; how to care for the possessions they already have; how to plan ahead so they are not constantly relying on your last-minute services; and how to practice reciprocal generosity toward you and the less fortunate. Teaching these lessons in self-restraint begins by asking yourself whether there are reasons you might secretly prefer not to.

BARRIERS TO TEACHING SELF-RESTRAINT

I once worked with a family who bought their daughter, Lily, a platinum BMW as a birthday surprise. The parents chose the make and color with care, imagining this safe and elegant car parked in front of their house. On the morning of her birthday, Lily looked through the window, saw the new car sitting outside with a big bow perched on top . . . and began to sob. When her parents asked her what was wrong, Lily said, "I don't want that car. I want a blue car."

Lily's parents were shocked at their daughter's ungracious response to their gift. They had bought her a solid and beautiful car that would take her through high school, college, and even beyond. When I asked Lily's parents to tell me more about Lily's reaction, however, a backstory emerged. Her mother explained:

Oh, Lily has this thing for blue. From the time she was small, when all the other girls were wearing pink or purple, Lily wore blue dresses to birthday parties. When she was six or seven she would say: "My eyes are cornflower, the midnight sky is indigo, and the water in the swimming pool is aquamarine." At this point, Lily's mother took a sharp breath inward. "Oh, no," she said. "I think I now understand why Lily started crying over her birthday present. I remember that as soon as she got her learner's permit she started talking about a blue car. I actually think she would have been happy with a used Honda Civic, as long as it was blue. But since we're a BMW family, we forgot about everything else."

It's possible to read Lily's reaction as bratty, spoiled teen behavior; a brand-new BMW, in any color, is more than most teenagers hope to receive. It's also possible to appreciate her commitment to self-expression. As her mother realized, Lily wasn't concerned with broadcasting her family's image. I've seen this parent-teen dilemma played out in a variety of ways: cars, clothes, college choices. How can teens learn a mature sense of self-restraint when parents not only buy them things to establish their own image but also hide that motive behind the excuse "We're just teaching you the importance of quality"?

Before you assume that your teen's sense of entitlement is solely her problem, take some time to reflect on your habits. Do you, like Lily's parents, buy your child expensive things to impress others in the community with your family's financial standing, and then brand her as shallow when she voices her own desires? Or have you stumbled into any of these other dead ends in the labyrinth of parents, teens, and money?

Buying affection

Your child, who once adored you, is now either distant and monosyllabic or theatrically miserable and critical. When the thread connecting you to your child feels thin, your inclination is to protect against stretching it further. You may purchase goods or services for your teens because you're afraid that if you don't, the thread will snap.

Vicarious pleasure

As we grow older, it's tempting to borrow self-esteem and vanity from the young. They look good in clothes; they can use expensive sports equipment with dash; their lives are rich and colorful. But it's demoralizing for teens to feel like they're your dress-up dolls or action figures.

Overextended compassion

When teenagers complain that "everyone else" has the "it" item or is signed up for a singular summer travel experience, they are really saying that the acquisition of these things will help them fit in with the popular kids or another tribal group. They are right: Teens do need certain tools to achieve social status. There are times when buying your teen the right brand of boots or the right bicycle is a respectful, compassionate approach. But be wary of teaching your teen that money can buy friends, or that their social needs justify straining the family's budget.

Overrewarding
An emphasis on product over process can lead good parents to practice a form of bribery: You hand me good grades, impressive sports achievements, enviable social status, or another fill-in-the-blank measure of success, and I'll buy you whatever you want. A steady diet of rewards can actually backfire and reduce intrinsic motivation. It also teaches teens that moderation is not an attribute of successful people.

The consumption mentality
When parents get in the habit of using shopping as a way to distract themselves from uncomfortable feelings, they discover that the pleasure quickly evaporates and the letdown leads to a craving for more narcotic shopping. If you habitually try to solve your teen's problems by buying her more stuff—more clothes, more electronics, more special trips— you may be passing this unsatisfying, ineffective problem-solving strategy down to your child.

Moral superiority
Allowing your teen to become a selfish and spoiled teenager allows you to feel martyred, indignant, injured . . . and morally superior. When your confidence is fragile, this superiority can give you a lift and additionally provide you and your spouse with constant conversational fodder: "I walked into the house and she didn't look up from the computer, didn't even nod. . . . And she wants new shoes for the semiformal? No way!" In the natural choreography of parent-teen frustrations, it's common to feel annoyed and even furious from time to time, but if you find yourself contemptuous of your child, it's time to get out of the boxing ring and into the office of a counselor or therapist.

TEACH YOUR TEEN TO BUDGET

One way to put the *yetzer* on a leash is to put your child in charge of paying for life's extras. Your teens can work for their spending money (an idea I endorsed in chapter 4), and most parents also give older children a regular allowance. The purpose of an allowance isn't to help your teen save for college or learn to give to charity. These goals are worthy but this kind of parsing of the budget is usually too cumbersome for adolescents to manage. Nor is an allowance payment for chores, because chores are best viewed as an essential aspect of family citizenship. The purpose of an allowance is simple: to teach teens how to budget for discretionary items.

What does an allowance cover? I like to put teens in charge of those expenses that require a steady drip of cash; gas, music and media purchases, and eating out with friends are some common examples. An allowance also gives you a way to reduce friction with your child. If you have arguments along the lines of "How can you possibly think you need another pair of Converse high-tops?" or "Do you really expect me to pay twenty-two dollars for lip gloss?," add nonessential wardrobe items and makeup to the list. Teens who have shown themselves capable of managing smaller amounts of money can be given allowances to cover more and bigger items, including musical instruments, sports equipment, the mobile phone bills, clothing basics, and haircuts.

An allowance (and a part-time job) should reduce the number of times you and your teen clash over money. When she begs for a discretionary item, you can remind her that she's responsible for it. The payment comes out of her own pocket.

SHOW RESPECT FOR THEIR DESIRES, BUT DON'T AUTOMATICALLY GIVE IN TO THEIR TERMS

The *yetzer hara* eats money for breakfast. The most generous allowance in the world won't stop your teen from begging you to buy something that is too expensive or unnecessary or duplicates something she already has. What's the best response to these requests? In the usual parental script, there are several popular but ineffective rhetorical ploys. You may even recall some of them from your own childhood:

Do you think I'm made of money?

There are at least a dozen purses stashed on the floor of your closet that you never even use. Why do you always want more and more and more? Can't you be grateful for what you already have?

Don't you ever think of anyone but yourself?

Did you hear that? The sound of your voice shouting into the wind? Remember that you're speaking to the *yetzer hara* here. The *yetzer*'s job is to crave status symbols and shiny things. It doesn't listen to reason, and it lashes out when attacked. You'll get better results by working with the *yetzer* instead of against it, so try empathizing with your teenager's desire for a new handbag without rushing out to buy one for her:

> Mom: *I hear you. I hear you. I know you really want a new bag. And your old one is looking a little tired. Let's figure out how you can get one.*
>
> Daughter *(sarcastically)*: *Um, let's see…you could go to the store and buy it for me?*
>
> Mom: *I can do that if we wait until your birthday. If you want it sooner, you can call the Roths or the Corwins about baby-sitting. Or use your birthday money from Grandma and Grandpa. If you pitch in half the money, and if the price is reasonable enough, I would be glad to cover the rest.*
>
> Daughter: *This is so unfair! Everyone else has a decent bag. Maddie has two Betsey Johnson clutches, Isabella has a new Coach wristlet, and Hannah has three Marc Jacobs, three, I saw them in her closet. This old piece of junk I'm forced to carry is (a) falling apart and (b) an embarrassment.*

At this point, your teen might stomp off, but she'll probably return shortly, after the storm has passed. She'll be less indignant but her desire will be intact.

> Daughter: *I called the Corwins and I'm baby-sitting on Saturday night from six to eleven or later! And they need me for a few hours on Wednesday after school to help*

> *Talia with her homework. I was planning to use my*
> *birthday money to see Plain White T's in concert, but*
> *I checked online and the tickets are only twenty dol-*
> *lars, so that leaves me with thirty extra. I found a*
> *little pink velour Juicy hobo for eighty dollars! Well,*
> *plus shipping and stuff. If you pitch in twenty dollars*
> *I can make it. I'd be so happy, Mom.*

Now is when parents are most likely to blow the negotiation, by say-ing:

I just bought you a new purse last month. What's wrong with that one?
Or:
Pink velour? Don't you think that will get dirty really fast? Juicy? Don't
those bags have a logo emblazoned in glitter across the whole front of the ugly
thing?
Or:
A little handbag? With all the junk you carry?

Resist saying any of these. Recall two things. One: Your daughter's craving for the Juicy bag is not about rationality or practicality. It's based on love. Yes, it's a recreational purchase but she's willing to work for it and to sacrifice some of her savings. Two: You already agreed to pitch in some money toward the handbag. Nothing is lost in this transaction but your twenty dollars; it's a cheap investment in keeping your word and respecting your teen's taste.

Not every teen request should result in a financial contribution from you. But thoughtfully working out the problem has a very, very differ-ent impact than consistently saying, "No, you already have a bag. Stop talking nonsense and leave me alone." Or whisking your child off to the department store and saying, "Here, love, take your pick." By turn-ing the main responsibility for a purchase back toward your teen, you deliver a lesson that is more far effective than pious speeches about grati-tude. Using this collegial approach ("Maybe we can figure out a way for you to get the bag if you spend your own money"), you give your teen a chance to learn. She may find that her desire for a couture handbag quickly evaporates once she is asked to come up with the money herself. Or if her desire lingers or grows, she'll discover the satisfaction of pro-ductively channeling her *yetzer* energy toward a chosen goal.

A final word on dealmaking with teens. You'll notice that in the dialogue above, the parent ignores the cheeky responses from her daughter. You can't force a teen to be gracious, although you can demonstrate through your own choice of words that graciousness is the ideal. But if your teen crosses the line:

I think you're suffering from dementia. Really. You told me you would buy me a new bag last week but there is nothing, nothing I would be willing to carry that costs as little as you're willing to spend. You actually promised me that I could get anything I wanted, but now you're forgetting on purpose. You forget everything that's important to me. This is not about a bag anyway. It's about basic respect and understanding. You don't care what I need. And you don't really care about me.

Do not debate the dementia (even if you're worried that she's right), the truth of the supposed "promise," or the alleged lack of love. Now is the time to walk away from the negotiating table. Say, "I can't talk to you when you're shouting at me. I can see that we're not going to agree on this right now, so let's close the subject. Maybe we can try again later." If your teen brings up the subject again, using a more respectful approach, you can restart the discussion.

MEDIA: THE THIRD PARENT

The formula for managing teenage materialism could be fairly straightforward: Teens want stuff; parents set aside a budget for stuff and require teens to cover extras with their own money. But there is another force at work. Media and advertisers operate like an alluring, wealthy, and uninvited third parent in your child's world, and the teen's *yetzer hara* is vulnerable to their wiles.

Advertisers spend billions of dollars a year marketing directly to children and teenagers. And they don't waste their money. The agencies spend more than any university psychology department to study the cognitive and emotional development of teenagers, and while their methods are sophisticated, their goal is simple: Create or exaggerate a problem (acne, lackluster hair, middling social status) and offer a simple solution (benzoyl peroxide, herbal-scented shampoo, sexy clothing). Teenagers, with their natural feelings of both inadequacy and idealism, are perfect targets for corporate seduction. "Ah, yes, if I only had X, I could become Y." It's impossible for parents to shield them from exposure to this emotional manipulation because it is ubiquitous.

The consumer message follows teens wherever they go. It's on television, of course, but also online. Identify yourself as female on Facebook and ads for fat-busters and teeth-whitening aids appear on your page. If you're male, ads pop up for wine coolers and online games. Teens see billboards on the way to school; they view ads before films; and at the mall, the goods for sale advertise themselves. While researching this topic, I learned that if you display T-shirts in the order of the colors of the rainbow, fewer will be sold than if you mix it up a bit. Teens are not safe from marketing even at school, where corporate logos appear on scoreboards, athletic equipment, and book covers. Corporate-sponsored school seminars, such as a program on self-esteem in which teens are given goodie bags filled with acne cream and deodorant, continue the barrage.

If parents don't offer their teens some lessons on marketing psychology, no one will. But you'll need to use a light touch. If you belittle your child's desire for designer sunglasses or denim leggings, you're not teaching a lesson in higher values. You're just revealing that you've forgotten how scary it is to be fifteen, to find yourself with oddly proportioned limbs or a nose that is too big for your face, and to hope that the right product will help you form a graceful package out of unharmonious parts. If you deliver a long lecture on the evils of advertising, your teenager will dismiss you as a pious killjoy—because, in truth, many of the products being sold to your teen are useful or fun, and some of the television ads are more entertaining than the shows.

A more effective approach begins with establishing yourself as a fellow traveler in the world of consumer delights. Share your pleasure in talented entertainers, well-crafted television plots, or beautiful merchandise showcased in wittily produced commercials. Join your teen in watching a rented comedy and say, "Zach Galifianakis is brilliant." When your daughter comes home from a shopping trip with an item she first saw advertised in her favorite magazine, say, "That dress is a winner."

Then, bit by bit, teach your child the ploys of advertising. Instead of sounding preachy, indignant, or smug, approach the subject as if you were a master detective passing on secrets of the trade. Appeal to your teen's intelligence and desire to be free of mind control. Show her the

T-shirt displays at the mall and talk about the color display trick. Watch the latest teen vampire love story and talk about how brand-name products are used to advance plots in a practice called "script integration." (Notice how often the vampire checks his smartphone.) Suggest counting the number of Volkswagens that appear during a movie and explain that car companies pay big money to slip their products into a film studio's productions. Don't bring up the subject too often, or your child will soon tune out your one-note song. But do let these conversations take on greater and greater depth as your teen grows older, and eventually she will mature in her ability to reflect and choose rather than react and spend.

WHEN THEY BREAK AND LOSE THINGS

Nearly every parent of a teenager has experienced a variation on this scene:

Mom is dressing to go out and finds that her favorite sweater is missing. When she locates the sweater crammed in the back of her daughter's middle drawer, she's exasperated. "You took my sweater?" she says. "You have so many nice sweaters, more than I do. Why can't you wear one of your own?"

Then the daughter responds, "Actually, I don't have any decent sweaters. Not one."

A thorough cross-examination reveals the condition and whereabouts of the daughter's sweaters. She took sweater A to camp in case she wanted to wear it to the dance but instead wore it to the campfire and got toasted marshmallow on it and then tried washing it in the camp laundry, where it got ruined. She loaned sweaters B and C to her friend Olivia, who might have loaned them to her friend Maya. No idea where sweater D is at present. Sweater E is dirty. Sweater F shrunk. There are, in fact, no wearable sweaters in the daughter's room.

One of the biggest gripes from parents is that teens don't take care of their possessions. The same teens who are so thrilled by shopping for just the right, coveted items will bring those items home and immediately start to mistreat them. The wise parent comes to know that this problem is too common and chronic to warrant the stress of daily bickering. Instead, adopt this radical philosophy: Once you have bought an item for your teen, or once the teen has purchased something with her own money, it belongs to her.

If you're frustrated by how often your teen is careless with her possessions, start by asking yourself whether she has the necessary knowledge and training to take care of her things properly. Teens can dazzle you with their sophisticated knowledge of number theory or the precise social hierarchy in the freshman class, but they may have never learned how to comb the fuzzy pills out of a sweater or that sports uniforms will get eaten by mold if left in a sweaty pile for too long. Now is the time to provide this information. Even if your teen is impatient while you explain about how to wash clothes by hand and how to dry a jacket so that it won't shrink, you are helping her build an arsenal of ordinary but essential life skills.

If you see your teen about to mistreat an object even after you've taught her how to care for it, recognize that adolescents have a lot on their minds. The maintenance of their possessions, even beloved ones, is not at the forefront of their thoughts. Nor are they mature enough to think about consequences that can occur tomorrow or next week or next month. A brief reminder about the possible effects of their actions is a kindness: "Lauren, I'm concerned that if you leave your bike outside all night, it might get stolen."

But be nonalarmist in your warnings, and remember that it's her stuff, not yours. If she loans her new black jacket to a friend, that's her business. (Teens, selfish as they act with you, will generously circulate their favorite possessions among their friends.) If he leaves his bicycle outside on the driveway and someone runs over it with a car in the dark, it's his problem. No matter how cheap or expensive the item, they own both it and the consequences. Don't lecture, scold, and then grudgingly buy a replacement. If you do, your child will learn that life is a drama in which others are always waiting in the wings, on hand to fix, repair, and replace the props they have broken. But if you let them make mistakes and then experience their consequences, reality will be their teacher. They will eventually learn to balance their impulsive *yetzer* with the cognitively mature habits of foresight, attention to detail, and good planning.

Encourage teens to fix their problems on their own, and be tolerant of screwball solutions. If your son comes up with a plan to make money to buy a new bike by selling origami birds, that's fine. If he wants to let a friend fix the bike in his parents' garage, that's also fine. You can be on hand to advise and assist as tolerated. But don't deprive your teen of this opportunity to develop resourcefulness. Of course, if your teen chronically loses or breaks her things, let her know that you will take this carelessness into consideration when making purchases in the future. If she takes your things and then mistreats them, she loses the privilege of borrowing your stuff.

MY PARENT, MY SERVICE PROVIDER

Mom, I need you to drive me to Alissa's party on Saturday night—and just drop me off in front of her house, okay? You don't need to stay around. Plan to pick me up at eleven.

Okay, I know I should have thought of this before, but I need to have my geology field notes folio-bound before class tomorrow. I called the copy store on Pine Street and they can do an express job for me for just fifteen dollars extra. Pine Street is on your way home from Lucy's ballet class, right? Can you drop the notes off and then stop by and pick them up for me? I'll pay you back later.

A teen's *yetzer hara* will make demands of you that are urgent, compelling, beautifully articulated, and offensive. You may find it hard to resist falling into the trap of resentful compliance: *Geology field notes. Those are important, right? Well, that's just great. I guess I have to do it for her.* It's a challenge to decide when to willingly provide services and when to calmly say no. Adolescents who don't learn how to set some limits on their requests of adults can, ironically, develop a bad case of anxiety and chronic discontent. They won't know how to plan ahead on their own or how to find satisfaction in ways that don't depend on the assistance of others.

I recommend treating a request for a service the same way you'd treat a request to buy something. If the request is reasonable, go ahead and fulfill it. If it's the result of a rarely occurring problem, consider it an opportunity to assist a deserving young person. But if the request is burdensome or caused by persistent procrastination or laziness, try coming to an alternate solution. This may mean allowing your teen to suffer the consequences of her poor planning—perhaps allowing her to take a grade reduction for the bound portfolio that she picks up late and pays for on her own. If your teen suffers from a severe, chronic case of service entitlement, an adjustment in your own attitude may yield some relief. You may be tempted to bond with a selfish teen by asking about his favorite topic—his troubles—but be wary of letting him think of himself as helplessly requiring your constant assistance. Consider this interchange:

> Mom: *Hi, honey. How did your day go? You seemed so tired out this morning. Let's make sure you get to bed on time tonight. Did you finish the Child Soldiers paper during your free period? Oh, and how's your foot? Did Mr. Mars let you sit out PE?*
>
> Son: *I don't feel great, actually. I'm still tired and my foot still hurts. But if you could pretty please run over to the library and find me a non-Web source for the paper, I might be feeling better by the time you get back.*

Now compare it to this one:

> Mom: *Hi, honey. How was your day? Wow, I had a long one, but it was good and tomorrow's Friday. So, how are you? How's the paper coming along?*
>
> Son: *Well . . . [he's considering asking his mother to visit the library for him but, having been told that her day was long, thinks better of it] . . . the paper is um, okay, but . . . I'm not finished yet. Could you take me to the downtown library after school tomorrow? I need one last non-Web resource for the bibliography.*

Note that the second mother's patter has a different flavor than the first. It's more mutual. Instead of leading with "How are you feeling?" she includes both her day and his project. It's warm and thoughtful, but it doesn't feed his self-centeredness by making his every possible concern the center of their shared world. It does not invite the child to take advantage of his mom. As parents, we can be simultaneously friendly *and* confident that our children do not constantly require our breathless assistance.

COUNTERBALANCE SELF-CENTEREDNESS
WITH COMMUNITY SERVICE

Community service provides a bracing antidote to adolescent self-centeredness. When teenagers serve others, the spotlight shifts away from them and onto the needs of someone else: a child who is still a halting reader in fourth grade or an elderly person who'd like help downloading pictures of his grandchildren. And when teenagers are digging, pulling weeds, washing, planting, hammering, mopping, cooking, reading, singing, or building, they have a chance to escape from themselves: from overthinking, from their self-preoccupation and their self-doubt. It's a relief.

Since most schools have community service requirements for graduation, the real question for parents is not whether to encourage their teen to do volunteer work but how to help them compare and evaluate the relative benefits of different service opportunities. Here are some ideas for choosing volunteer work that will help your child decenter:

Avoid shallow "service gestures"
Earlier, I warned that college admissions officers see through service trips to Africa or other exotic locations, which are often little more than heavily chaperoned cultural tourism. Phony service opportunities exist closer to home, too, so watch out for them. At one high school, students received community service credit just for bringing in used cell phones. It was a valuable contribution, but one requiring little effort. Elsewhere, students signed up to paint a shelter for unwed mothers. Upon arrival they were served big deli sandwiches and cookies. They were not asked to mask the molding or ceiling or window frames with tape; instead, the students casually slathered the paint on the walls with wide brushes. They had lots of opportunity to chat and gossip and had a really fun afternoon. As the school bus pulled away, a crew of professional painters arrived to do the real work. In the end, the project was hollow because it was only about the teens—about fulfilling their community service requirement, about an afternoon of fun—and not about service to or sacrifice for others.

Encourage person-to-person weekly service

The richest kind of volunteer work involves building personal relationships over time. My psychologist colleagues and I know that among the many pleasures of doing psychotherapy is the opportunity to be lifted out of your own concerns during the clinical hour. The regularity of the meeting time, the privilege of the client's trust in you, and the opportunity to concentrate on someone else's needs in a very focused manner for a brief but intense period of time are all transporting. When a teenager provides service to the same people from visit to visit he will, like a psychotherapist, first be required to learn how to speak the other person's language: to figure out through trial and error how to communicate with someone whose whole style of interaction—vocabulary, habits, pace, and tempo—will be new to him. Once a relationship has been built, the responsible child will honor a commitment to this person or people who now know him, remember him, and expect him to show up to provide them with assistance and companionship.

When the child your teen is tutoring tells her that his brother has been sent to Iraq, or the elderly adult he visits finally learns how to send e-mail or a photo attachment, your child is removed from his own narrow sphere of preoccupations. The meta-meaning of recent text messages, or his worries about how he'll do on his upcoming history final, move out of the forefront of his thoughts for a time. For a short while, he learns what it feels like to be free of self-absorption.

Of course, not every teen has the time for this level of commitment. Short-term but absorbing service projects, such as collecting old and broken bicycles, repairing them, and delivering them to the boys' club, are still of value. "I helped some kids today. Mom, one of those boys *cried* when he saw the bikes."

Send them outside their comfort zone

Saying "yes" to service projects in unfamiliar settings counterbalances prejudice and negative assumptions:

When I first got to the retirement home I hated the smell and all the people sat in chairs like zombies, then I met Al and we had a really great conversation about the first big-band concert he ever went to. And a lady, who has a number tattooed on her arm, told us about how her sister was sent from Germany to England with a bunch of other kids when she was only six.

Let them get dirty

Many community service activities are low tech, gritty, and refreshingly wholesome. At the end of a day spent hoeing hard soil for a community garden or harvesting zucchini, or cleaning up a mile-long stretch of beach, scratched palms and sore backs are the badges your child will wear for making a real contribution. In "dirtier" community service, what do teenagers earn? The knowledge that they are sturdier than they imagined, that the safe world is wider and more interesting than they knew, and that what sometimes seems daunting or dangerous or beyond their ability is within their reach.

Let your teen volunteer with other teens

Volunteering as a family is an example of what psychologists call "maximizing"—a nice idea that's often too bulky and cumbersome to coordinate successfully. Teens enjoy volunteer work with an edge (a power tool, dirt, a new neighborhood) or special sentiment (singing together while painting a playground, tenderly caring for animals). With their parents around, the thrill can be diluted or exuberant expressions of love and tenderness can be stifled by self-consciousness.

HEALTHY NARCISSISM IN PARENTS

Bad old joke: How many Jewish mothers does it take to screw in a light-bulb?

None, I'm fine. I'll just sit here in the dark.

Sacrifice on behalf of your children is central to the job description, but effective parenting does not include neglecting yourself. Are your clothes faded and dated while your teen's are fresh and new? Do you ferry your children to daily sports practices while neglecting your doctor's recommendation to get thirty minutes of exercise on most days of the week? Do you perform major services for your teens even when you are sick or exhausted? If your family's resources run only in one direction, from parent to child, it's time to reverse the flow a little.

Require Assistance from Your Teens

Assisting you will probably not come naturally to teens, so plan to teach them how. Show them how to prepare food and drink for themselves and explain that they should offer you some of it, too. This could be as rudimentary as pouring sodas into cups over ice or as complicated as making a multicourse dinner. Require help with your "homework"—addressing envelopes, putting in new shelf paper for the cabinets, or picking up batteries (*Pay attention: We need triple A, not double A*) from the store. When you are sick, let your teen play nursemaid by bringing you tissues or hot tea. When you're getting ready for a trip, ask your teen to carry your suitcase down the stairs even if you're strong enough to do it yourself. It's more important for you to give them an opportunity to assist you than to demonstrate your youthful vigor. Don't expect that your teen will do all things with skill or enthusiasm, not at first. But if you require teens to help you anyway, they will eventually learn to perceive the needs of others, even through their haze of hormones, emotions, and alienation.

Dress Yourself Nicely

There are compelling reasons to spend money on clothes for your children instead of yourself. They are forever outgrowing their clothes and thus are in constant need of new jeans, new shoes, new coats. They need certain items to fit in at school; they need sleek and sparkly things to wear to the prom. For some parents, but certainly not all, it becomes a habit to buy for the children and deny themselves, especially as middle age creeps in and the cruel fluorescent lights and elongating mirrors of a department store fitting room make it hard to trust what you see, to feel secure, to make a good decision about what looks good on you.

But what reason do teens have to leave behind their immaturity and become adults if their parents look shabby and neglected? Jewish tradition tells us that there is no piety in self-denial and looking run-down; the great Jewish philosopher and rabbi Moses Maimonides wrote that no scholar should live in a town without a perfumery and a shop for baskets. Inoculate your teen against entitlement by giving yourself a small dose. Devote a reasonable portion of the household budget to your own appearance, to nice clothes and good grooming. Even if they insult your taste, your children will be encouraged when they see that you feel dignified and worthy enough to take care of yourself.

TRIAL, ERROR, AND GOOD DEPRIVATION

Constant fulfillment of desire is the enemy of both satisfaction and grati-tude. A 1999 Alfred P. Sloan Foundation study of adolescent satisfaction confirms this observation.* The findings revealed that adolescent happi-ness varies *inversely* with parental income. Children from working-class homes report the highest level of happiness, while upper-middle-class children report the least. The reasons? Privileged children, deprived of deep longing, consequently are deprived of deep satisfaction.

This philosophy of "good longing" is easy to describe but difficult to practice. How does a mother know when her teen would benefit from good deprivation and when to take a more generous approach—to sup-ply goods, run errands, and smooth over problems? Let's visit with a twelfth grader on an important day in her life.

It's three o'clock in the afternoon, time for Lana to get dressed to leave for graduation ceremonies. But when she goes to the closet to get the dress she and her mother purchased at Banana Republic for the occa-sion, Lana finds a miniature version on the hanger. Soon she realizes what has happened. After Lana wore the new dress to a dance last week ("Just once before graduation, I mean it, only once, it's so pretty!"), she came home late and left the dress on the floor before flopping into bed. On Wednesday morning, after being reminded by Mom that the house-keeper was coming in later that day, Lana chucked a big pile of clothes into the hamper before rushing off to school. The dress got washed with the darks, whereupon it shrunk. Lana's only other graduation outfit option? An old dress, one that was not dressy or special or new.

What does "Mom A" do? When Lana comes downstairs in an old dress and explains what happened to the new one, Mom A does not mention Lana's appearance at all but gives her glum-looking daughter a hug, tells her how proud she is to see her graduating. But what she's thinking is:

Clearly this girl hasn't yet learned to check that she has everything she needs before a big event . . . or to hang up good clothes rather than leaving them on the floor. Clearly it's time for her to start doing her own laundry. I'm going to require her to pay me back for the dress with her baby-sitting money and close

---

*Suniya S. Luthar and Bronwyn E. Becker, "Privileged but Pressured? A Study of Affluent Youth," *Child Development* 73:5 (October 2002): 1593–1610.

her iTunes and school store account until she proves herself more responsible.
She is so careless with the things we buy her, but she always expects us to replace
what she ruins. No more. It's too much.

"Mom B" also gives her sad-looking daughter a hug. "It's okay,
Mom," the girl says. Mom B then calls every Banana Republic in the
area, finds the same dress in the right size, races through a huge, unfamiliar mall to retrieve the dress, politely inquires if the sales associate
would be willing to steam the dress to get the wrinkles out, cuts off the
tags, races back through the mall, and drives back just in time for Lana
to change and hop into the car for the ceremonies. Lana is so grateful
that her eyes well up with tears.

There is no single correct response to the dress situation. While each
day spent parenting a teenager invites you to develop the story of your
child, a case file on her character, no single incident is a measure of her
maturity or whether or not you have spoiled her. You can decide when
to be parent A or B (or C, or D . . .) by evaluating the duration, intensity,
and frequency of your child's demands for goods, services, and rescue.
Mom A weighed her daughter's chronic lack of responsibility and "buy
me this, buy me that" attitude. For this mother, the graduation debacle
was the last straw. In contrast, Mom B appreciated that her daughter
seemed to accept responsibility for her situation. Mom B thought: *She*
doesn't have many party dresses, and she never complains about wearing the
same things over and over. It's graduation! Why not try to help out?

Consider where you fall both in the crunch and on a typical day. Run
a test on your resentment barometer. Is your child suffering from oversatiation of desire, or does she fall within the limits of normal teenaged
lust for stuff? Is she demanding of assistance in a tight spot, or grateful
for it? If you have never once performed the equivalent of Mom B's frantic dash through the mall, your child may consider your consistent lack
of compassion as evidence of her own unworthiness. If you're *always*
running through the mall, you are not helping your child grow but are
crippling her with kindness and caring. You may read this and worry:
Oh, no, I've been acting like Mom B when my child is daughter A! But mistakes are proper and good. Just as teens learn by trial and error and error
and error, so do their parents.

Generally with teens, less is more. Use whatever mantra helps you to
say no to over-the-top entitlement. *Creativity blossoms when it faces limits.*

A sonnet is fourteen lines, a haiku just three. When water is allowed to sprinkle it loses pressure, but when it is channeled through a hose the flow is more powerful. Or think of this *New Yorker* cartoon: A mother looks at her teenaged daughter, who sits on a floor strewn with an electric guitar, ball of yarn and needles with a few inches knitted, computer, two books, and an easel. Caption: "Maybe if your creativity had fewer outlets, it would come out of you with more force."

Yet keep in mind that teens need to be narcissistic in order to separate from you and create a new self. Look again at some select details of the definition of narcissistic personality disorder: a sense of self-importance; fantasies about success, power, brilliance, beauty, or ideal love; belief in being "special" and unique. Good traits for a blossoming young person, within limits.

CHAPTER 6

The Blessing of Problems to Solve:

Letting Your Teen Learn from Bad Judgment and Stressful Situations

College deans use the code name "teacups" for incoming students who are overprotected and fragile. When presented with a challenge, teacups don't rise to it. They crack:

My drunk roommate and her boyfriend come in at two a.m. every night and get in her bed. I just cover my head with my pillow and feel like crying.

I've been getting sandwiches at Subway for dinner and eating in my room every night because I feel funny walking into the dining hall alone. But now I think that the people who work there think I'm this pathetic, weird girl, so I'm just getting ramen from the student store and heating it in the microwave. For lunch I have a Lara bar.

I don't think I should be in Spanish III. It's too hard. Talking to the professor won't help, I know it.

I thought about working for the arts magazine but I went to the first meeting and the kids were not my type. I'm not going back. I'm fine just chilling in the dorm and playing Splinter Cell.

Shocked and paralyzed when asked to navigate unfamiliar situations, teacups end up in the health center with headaches, stomachaches, insomnia, and eating disorders. They isolate themselves from other students, hunkering down in their dorm rooms between classes, or they burn themselves out with overwork. An increasing number of college freshmen are returning home after the first semester, unable to cope. A young woman I know called her mother a few days after school started, sobbing, "You need to come get me because the bathrooms are gross. I think there's mold growing between the floor tiles." In her case, a moldy bathroom, so easily remedied with a little bleach and water or simply ignored, was a metaphor for a world in which no one was making sure her surroundings were clean and safe and protected. A few weeks later, she returned home for good.

How can we avoid sheltering our kids into such a dangerous state of fragility? If we want to raise young adults who know how to solve problems, we must let them have problems to solve while they are still adolescents. Yet it's harder and harder to find parents willing to expose their children to difficulty. More often, parents keep their teens busy in adult-supervised activities so there is no time for trouble, or rush in to solve problems instead of leaving the solution in their teens' shaky hands. If Mom thinks that Kayla's boyfriend isn't good enough for her, she steps in with unsolicited advice and might even call around town to find a better one. If Jack is afraid to raise his hand in geometry class and ask the teacher to explain concepts he doesn't understand, his parents hire a friendly tutor to come to the house after school. When Ariella has her second fender bender in the school parking lot, her parents pay for the damage to both cars and let stressed-out Ariella skip Grandma's birthday party to soothe her nerves with a soak in the tub. Daniel's parents won't let him drive at night because *who knows* what kind of crazies might be out there?

It would be cruel for parents to abandon their teens to the trials of adolescence without any protection at all. But it is also unfair to lead teens to believe they are too weak or too delicate to learn how to sustain themselves emotionally, mediate disputes, tolerate unfamiliar situations, and negotiate bureaucracies. How to strike the right balance between appropriate guidance and restraint? The story of the Israelites' trip out of slavery in Egypt offers some clues.

The book of Exodus describes the quality of God's presence during the Israelites' travels as a "pillar of cloud by day . . . and a pillar of fire by night." This beautiful image is a model for parents whose children are wandering in the wilderness of adolescence. Like God, you stand by, providing shade and light when needed, but mostly you stand back. You detach. You wait to see if your child can solve problems on his own before stepping in; you let him experience the natural consequences of his poor decisions; and you give him the freedom to make mistakes, even big ones.

GIVE THEM GOOD SUFFERING

If we want children to learn the skills of independent living and to acquire good judgment *before* they leave home, they need to experience "good suffering" now. This means that parents shouldn't shield their children from the uncomfortable but normal problems of adolescence. When the parents I counsel ask me, "What should I do about those bitchy girls in my daughter's history class? The biology teacher who gives too much homework? The coach who cut my son from the team? My daughter's panic over her final exams?" I typically reply, "Don't do anything right away. Give the problem a chance to unfold naturally; give your child a chance to work things out for herself."

It's good for adolescents to be bored, lonely, disappointed, frustrated, and unhappy. It's good for them to have a crabby, unenlightened, uninspired history teacher. It's good for girls to have a shallow, domineering, slutty best friend. It's good for them to sit on the bench sometimes and even to have their hearts broken.

Why? Because you can be certain that in college they will have a shallow, domineering, slutty roommate or that one day they will have a crabby, unenlightened, uninspired professor or boss. Because as adults they will face serious disappointments, both professional and personal. Because we want them to learn as early as possible how to deal with difficult people and difficult emotions. Because by the time kids leave home, we want them to be familiar with the wave pattern of feelings: *I was feeling bad, but now, because I talked to my friend/went running/spoke to my professor/got some sleep/confronted my roommate about her boyfriend sleeping over/wrote up a plan to improve my soccer skills/went to the health center/actually finished some of my work, I notice that I feel better, and my parents had nothing to do with it.*

When we intervene to prevent the pain of tough situations, we create a reflex: Whenever the child feels any sadness or confusion, frustration or disappointment, she believes she cannot survive the feeling. If teenagers don't have an opportunity to recognize their bad feelings or problems and learn to manage them, they go off to college and seek out quick, reliable methods to make the pain disappear—meaning they substitute denial, alcohol, drugs, sex, dramatic relationships, frantic overwork, or daily calls home for actual problem solving.

Of course, teenagers will not make it easy for you to let them experience problems. Teenagers act as if they want to be independent, but they are actually adept at inflating their dilemmas into crises so that Mom and Dad will protect them:

How could Mr. Kornfield expect us to study for a test when he forgot to remind us it was coming up? If you won't talk to Kornfield for me, I'm going to ask Coach Martin to do it. No, I can't possibly study during free period! I have so many other things to do. There's absolutely no time. I have yearbook meetings and language lab and I assume you want me to have some lunch, don't you?

Mom, I just can't get over that Dylan is going out with Becca now. I think I've been crying for two hours. You can't expect me to go out and baby-sit with these red eyes. It's too embarrassing and, also, I'm sure that if Mr. and Mrs. Lane bring up anything at all that reminds me of what's going on in my life right now I'll start crying right there in their front hallway. I need to stay in my bedroom and be by myself for a while. Can you please call the Lanes and tell them I can't baby-sit tonight?

If you are going to successfully contain your impulse to fix and soothe, to let self-deluding or dramatic adolescents ride out their problems, you'll need to have some strategies at the ready.

Wait It Out

Teenagers' problems can catch fire, flare spectacularly, and then fizzle out just as quickly. Carol Eliot, a longtime seventh-grade teacher at an all-girls middle school, told me that mothers frequently phone her about the social drama between the girls: "Johanna is just devastated by what Lindsay and Alexandra have done to her!" Carol says she has learned to listen but not rush in. "By the time I start researching the problem, it's blown over. The girls say, 'What are you talking about?'"

If parents communicate anxiety in response to normal teen experiences—"That's awful! I thought Lindsay was a friend you could trust!" "How dare Mr. Singer assign you to third chair in the orchestra when he knows that the only reason you had trouble with your audition piece was that you were overtired?"—they suggest that there is no room for life's natural ups and downs. An overly anxious reaction on your part can also teach teens that you can't handle their distress, confusion, or poor choices, and they may become cautious about opening up to you in the future.

Be Empathic, Not Entangled

Although you shouldn't vibrate like an emotional tuning fork when your child brings you his troubles, avoid the opposite extreme of dismissing his emotions. When I asked two nineteen-year-olds how their parents could have helped when they were fourteen and suffering from heartaches, they said, "Don't say, 'You weren't really in love anyway. You're too young for that.'" I also caution parents against saying things like, "Stop moping about not making the team. Varsity soccer wasn't a good activity for you anyway. Come out of your room right now and I'll tell you why."

Instead, demonstrate empathy while avoiding entanglement in their disappointments. Be curious and kind, but unalarmed. You can say, *Ouch!* Or *Ow!* or *Oh!* Or *I can hear how troubled/upset you are by this.* Or *How confusing this seems.* Mostly listen and give your teen an opportunity to vent and unload. If you are asked for help directly, use leading questions that suggest your faith in her ability to mobilize her resources: *How are you considering handling that?* Or *What are you planning to try? What have you tried? How did it work? What's next?* Do your best to let the teen provide the answers on her own.

What if your teen is in obvious pain but doesn't want to share his sorrow with you? Some teens, often boys, respond to disappointment with a show of stoicism. It's such a painful sight—often worse than a girl's dramatic wailing—that parents can feel driven to prevent disappointment from ever touching their son again. Try taking a less direct approach with these buttoned-down souls. You can't force your son to talk, but you can prepare food for him, offer to drive him places, do chores in the same room he's in, or offer to shoot some hoops, so that if he does pitch you a ball of conversation, you'll be there to catch it. Then you can offer the same combination of empathy and confidence that you'd give to a more voluble teen.

Normalize Setbacks

When the drama has settled and your teen's feelings are less raw, let her know that setbacks are normal: Talk to teens about times when things didn't work out for you as you planned, how you coped, and what eventually came of the situation.

Encourage Them to Enlist the Aid of Other Adults

College administrators frequently complain that when teens have relatively small problems, their parents intervene at a very high level. The students seem unable or unwilling to work out their difficulties at the ground level, by talking to their professors or resident advisers or even going to see a doctor at the health center when they are sick. These administrators point out that kids who have learned to connect with nonparental adults fare much better in college than those who depend solely on their parents for assistance.

Teach your adolescent that adults actually enjoy helping those who ask respectfully and in a timely fashion. For some teens this means seeking out a mentor in a coach, a parent of a friend, or a member of the clergy. But because a teen's world is centered around school, many problems arise there, and these problems can often be managed by talking directly to a teacher. Your child may feel that this is awkward or embarrassing. He may ask you to circumvent whatever problem is occurring in class by hiring a tutor instead. But relying on a tutor your mom hired is different from negotiating your own relationship with a teacher. Kids who know that their own private grown-up will show up at their house at exactly four-thirty p.m. don't need to build up the confidence to talk to a busy teacher after class about the homework load or raise their hand and say, "Ms. Webber, I don't understand. Can you please explain that again?"

To a child who is resistant to talking with his teacher, you can say: "Students who go to see the teacher (I know it's hard) do better (I know it's hard) because the teacher knows they care (I know it's hard)." Even if your child absolutely refuses to ask an adult for help, you've planted the possibility in his mind. Come freshman or sophomore year of college, the seed may start to sprout.

Demonstrate Confidence in Your Teen's Problem-Solving Skills

When a teen has an acute problem, it's easy for parents to jump in, because we are experienced. We assume we know exactly how to repair the situation with minimum discomfort to all parties involved. Before you swing into action, allow your teen to surprise you with his resourcefulness. Many of the problems that trouble parents of teenagers will resolve themselves if you simply demonstrate confidence that your teen can handle them. A typical scenario:

Two days after getting a new car, Gabe calls his mother. "I'm completely lost," he says. "I'm almost out of gas and I don't think the neighborhood I'm in is a good one."

Gabe's mother, Sheila, says, "It's okay. Stay calm. Drive to the nearest intersection, pull over, and tell me the street names. Make double sure your doors are locked. We're on our way in the SUV. You know how safe it is—it's like an armored truck—and I'll drive you home while Dad takes your car to the gas station and fills up the tank."

In the SUV, Gabe says to his mother, "I told you I need an iPhone with maps!" Sheila buys one for him the next day.

Sheila had the best intentions, but she jumped in to rescue Gabe without considering first whether he was capable of saving himself. Here's how Sheila could have let the situation unfold:

> Gabe: *Mom, I'm completely lost. I'm almost out of gas and the neighborhood I'm in looks pretty scary.*
>
> Mom (taking a deep breath): *I don't know if they told you about this in driving school, but if you run out of gas completely it can damage the engine of the car. You'll need to find a gas station before you head home.*
>
> Gabe (indignant): *Mom! I told you I needed a GPS.*

Twenty minutes later, Gabe arrives home. His gas tank is full.

> Mom: *Gabe, good to see you. So how did it go after we talked on the phone?*
>
> Gabe: *Oh, I asked someone where a gas station was. Then I asked the people at the gas station for directions to the boulevard and I also remembered that I had a map in the car.*

Raising teenagers to develop life skills and street smarts—their own internal global positioning system—requires huge helpings of *bitachon,* both trust in God and trust in God's children. In this context, *bitachon* means you do your part, actively and responsibly, to advise or assist your child, but no more.

It also means that if your child does not solve a problem as well as you'd hoped, you resist interpreting the results as a divine judgment of your parenting skills. Have faith that your child can mine the experience for the value in it, and for guidance in the future.

Distinguish Dramas from Emergencies

When I first heard the GPS story, I thought about how Sheila acted on the assumption that her son's life was in immediate jeopardy, when actually he was a big, strong boy who had not wandered very far from his neighborhood. How does a parent distinguish between a genuine crisis that requires immediate intervention and a situation that is merely uncomfortable?

With young children, I recommend that parents confine the designation of "emergency" to three situations: when blood is running down fast; when the child has a high fever; or if there is a broken bone. Physical danger, or its immediate possibility, remains a good guideline for parents of teenagers. With teens, you know you've got a true emergency on your hands if the most sensible course of action is to call 911. House on fire? Car accident? Physical assault? Alcohol poisoning? You intervene. Do what needs to be done and call for help without hesitation. Also make it clear that your teen can always call on you in situations that hover just below the 911 range: if the only ride home from a party is with a drunk driver; if she's dumped in an unfamiliar neighborhood late at night by prankster friends; if he cuts his foot open while dancing barefoot in his girlfriend's backyard.

When your child is pleading for you to get him out of a bad situation but the danger factor is unclear, consider his voice or demeanor. When people are in a true emergency—the London bombings during World War II, a big Southern California earthquake, a bad car accident—they become quiet and still. Their voices drop. The blood drains from their faces and they turn pale. They don't exaggerate. But when people are inflating a situation to enhance its potential for drama, they do the opposite. They lay it on thick, they scream, they turn red, they blabber, they run about. If your child is yelling theatrically from his cell phone, consider the possibility that the situation may not be as dire as it appears to him at the moment. If he is turning gray or speaking in a hushed voice, consider that he may need your help even if he's not asking for it directly.

WHEN THEY CREATE THEIR OWN PROBLEMS, LET THEM EXPERIENCE THE CONSEQUENCES

Good suffering means not putting a barrier between our kids and the people or situations that can cause problems for them. The very best suffering occurs when we let kids experience the full weight of problems they create for themselves. Here's an inspiring exchange I heard about from a school principal:

Jake, a tall, athletic eleventh grader, was entertaining himself by throwing his car keys on the roof of the school building and listening to their musical clatter as they fell to the pavement below. This continued until the unlucky throw that caused the keys to get stuck.

Jake rushed into the principal's office to report the situation: "Mr. McIntyre, my keys are on the roof! Can you please call the maintenance crew so they can put up a ladder and get them down right away? I have a practice at four."

Mr. McIntyre replied calmly, looking up from his desk. "No can do. It's after hours for the maintenance crew. But in the spring they'll be clearing out the rain gutters. I'm sure your keys will turn up then."

"But Mr. M., this is not a joke. I'm in the starting line-up. And I saw Pete working near the toolshed just a few minutes ago. Can't you call him, please?"

When Mr. McIntyre pleasantly refused, Jake called his father. To his great irritation, his dad laughed. "Mr. McIntyre is a braver man than I am," he said. "I'm sure you can figure something out."

Eventually, Mr. McIntyre gave Jake permission to borrow the keys to the maintenance shed. Jake unlocked the shed, climbed the ladder he found there, and, with much grunting and straining, got the keys. He arrived late to the practice, and the coach penalized Jake by bumping him from the first quarter of Friday evening's game. To Mr. McIntyre's knowledge, Jake has never played key-toss roulette again.

I enjoy telling this story not only because it's an example of a father supporting a school administrator's decision, but also because Jake's dad is right: Allowing teens to live with the consequences that flow from their bad judgment requires a stout heart. Many teenagers, especially, but not exclusively, girls, see life as theater, and they will deftly cast you in a supporting role. If you do not play along by rescuing them from their procrastination or thoughtlessness or whatever trouble they're in, you risk being cast as the villain—neglectful, heartless, or in treacherous denial about the urgency of the drama:

You don't understand how important this paper is. It counts for half, Mom, half the grade. And Ms. Nash is such a bad teacher. Everyone knows it. She doesn't explain anything. And I couldn't even study at all last week because I had rehearsals and Morgan's party on Saturday. If I have to write the whole thing tonight I will fail, I know I will. All you have to do is let me stay home tomorrow to work on it. You can write the school saying I was sick. It's the only fair thing to do.

Boys have a different technique. They set out land mines of shock and righteous outrage:

We had no idea the volleyball net would catch on fire. I don't see why the park council should expect Garrett and me to pay for a replacement. They should have put a warning sign on it or something.

Or simply:

It's called Steal This Book, *so I stole it.*

While it is standard practice for teenagers to try to maneuver out of the unpleasant results of their procrastination or thoughtlessness, a parent's responsibility is to resist these tactics. If you play the role of your child's defense attorney, you preempt a process that is of value to them. You cut off the opportunity for reflection, regret, remorse, and learning about what not to do next time.

My friend's father used to say to his five children, "Well, I see you've gotten yourself into a fine fix this time. It's going to be interesting to see how you get yourself out of it." Both the fine fixes and their resolutions belong to our children, not to parents. By practicing respectful detachment, we are allowing teenagers a basic human right—to learn from their mistakes while they are still at home and before they set out for the wider world.

BUT IT'S TOO DANGEROUS!

We should avoid jumping in to save our children from problems, but we also need to allow them enough freedom to make mistakes, even big ones.

To drive this point home, I frequently begin my lectures by asking my audience about their own adolescent experiences: *When you were a young teenager, how many of you were allowed out until dark without your parents knowing where you were?* Almost every hand goes up.

And how many of you did things your parents never knew about?

Nearly everyone raises their hand. The audience laughs.

And still don't?

Same.

I see you survived. Did you have a good time?

Nods and smiles.

Then I ask them how many of their young teens are allowed to go anywhere, anytime without letting their parents know where they are. Not one hand is raised.

Today we view the high jinks, mischief, and dangerous adventures of our youth as anachronistic. I talk to parents about their adolescent thrills, and they beam with pride as they describe lying on the railroad tracks, cutting class, lying about their whereabouts, or accidentally blowing up a corner of the garage . . . but then they say some version of: "Oh, sure, that stuff was fine in a simpler world, in the old days, but not today. The world is so much more dangerous now!"

There's fallout from depriving kids of freedom, even if it's the freedom to do stupid things behind your back, like lie on the tracks and blow things up. Not only do our children lose the opportunity for excitement and adventure, they miss out on a crucial chance to develop good judgment. College deans and upperclassmen who deliver the "how to stay safe" lectures to freshmen have told me that they worry most about the students who were overprotected in high school. "Who's most at risk for all kinds of trouble?" one dean at a private college told me. "The kids who've been watched every moment of their lives, who have never taken a drink, never broken a rule, never been allowed out of the house without their cell phone." These are the kids prone to taking risks that are foolhardy and dangerous, because they've never learned what happens when you take smaller ones.

In Praise of Experience

When parents tell me "The world has changed. It used to be safer; now we can't take any chances," I respond with this story from my own youth:

One August day, the summer I was a junior camp counselor, my friend Patty and I stood at the side of a country road with our thumbs out. After waiting a few minutes longer than usual for someone to pick us up, we hesitated only slightly before getting into a car driven by a teenage boy. Did we care that there were three more boys in the car? No, we did not. Did we take into account that we could smell beer even from where we stood? Didn't give it much thought. It was our day off. It was hot. Very cold peanut butter milkshakes were to be had at the Dairy Den in town. A ride was a ride. When the driver headed down an isolated, winding road, Patty questioned him about the route.

"It's a shortcut," he said.

Then all the boys laughed.

I shoved Patty's head in my lap and said, "Uh-oh! Here she goes again. Open the windows all the way. Sometimes air helps. When her shoulders start heaving, it's usually too late. It's the curves in the road. They always make her really sick. We still haven't gotten the smell out of my father's car. Probably never will."

The boys ordered us out of the car immediately and sped away. I'm sure they talked all the way home about *their* narrow escape. We walked back to camp, repeating "Ohmygod" over and over.

As a team, we saved ourselves from a potential nightmare. Patty is a good navigator—I had no idea which road led in or out of town—and I'm a good improviser. In truth Patty never gets carsick. That day we pooled our skills and grew up a bit. We were naive and careless when we got into the car and more worldly when we got out. We had learned a lesson in the trenches.

I am not advocating that you seek out a program called "Adirondack Hitchhiking Adventures" as a summer enrichment experience for your child. Certainly none of the adults in my life would have allowed me to hitchhike if they had known about it. But Patty and I had what most teens today never get: the freedom to make a big mistake, to find ourselves in a dangerous situation and then save ourselves by teaming up and thinking fast.

Yes, the world has changed, but not all that much. What has changed is that when Patty and I were counselors, parents weren't constantly checking their e-mail for updates about sexual predators living in or near the camp's zip code, or texting back and forth with their kids about the day's agenda. Instead, our parents dropped us off for six weeks at camp, with a few instructions to be good and have a good time. This was *bitachon* in action.

Take a moment to remember your own youth: the company you kept, the laws you broke, the neighborhoods you hung out in, the shady moves, the secrets and lies. Remember your close calls and what you learned from them about etching a line between alluring and unsavory companions, an exciting caper and a criminal record, between procrastination and a really bad grade, and all the situations where you said to yourself, *Whoa, close call, I'll never do that again.* You matured and grew wiser. And here you are, decades later, mostly in one piece, comfortable in a well-lighted room, reading a parenting book.

Now it's time to give your teenager the opportunity to locate some boundaries on their own, the same way you did. Yes, adolescents are naive and grandiose, and parents have to help them judge and manage danger. But experience remains the best way to learn, and the only way your child can learn is if they are allowed to have some experiences. If we erect "Danger/Keep Out!" signs in front of the normal way stations of adolescent lives, we are creating a new danger for our children: the danger of excessive fearfulness.

The Mean World Syndrome

I meet many parents who agree with the need for freedom on principle, but are still paralyzed with worry about the dangers of today's world. Today, they argue, teens who step out after dark for a moment might be gone forever, abducted by molesters; boys who love violent video games are developing their inner Dylan Klebold; middle school girls wearing low-rise jeans are performing oral sex on boys under the table at bar mitzvahs; and all walks in the woods lead straight to Lyme disease.

Every one of these outcomes is possible but not likely. It's difficult to avoid worrying about low probability but highly sensational or exaggerated events because there are so many juicy media stories about them. The more vivid, bloody, sexy, and potentially fatal the activity, virus, or threat, the more people will tune in. Fear is compelling, and these images and stories make the danger seem real and close. The price we pay for focusing so much of our attention on terrible possibilities is what University of Pennsylvania researcher George Gerbner calls the "mean world syndrome." Gerbner found that the more news media or television people watch, the more they feel a pervasive sense of insecurity and vulnerability, the more reticent they are about going out on the street in their community, especially at night, and the more afraid they are of strangers and meeting other people. It's an infection. News becomes not just a window on the world but the world itself.

Television is not the only medium that whips us into a frenzy of overprotection. Magazines, radio broadcasts, the Internet, and nervous relatives and friends all give us information we can use to creatively imagine dangers to our children. I used to subscribe to a service provided by my local police department called "e-policing" that alerted me every time there was a crime in my neighborhood. When I realized that this information caused me to feel nervous all the time in a neighborhood that I know to be statistically very safe, I unsubscribed from the e-mail feed. But the inducements to worry are hard to avoid. Even without e-policing, you open your e-mailbox and find that your mother, or aunt, or hypervigilant friend has forwarded a warning about the hidden dangers of parking in public lots, of football playing on a teenager's growing skeletal structure, of not hiring a private college placement adviser. You stop whatever you're doing to weigh the info: Is it an urban legend or a legitimate scientific finding? Overblown or reasonable? Should I hire the tutor, forbid football, disallow my teenager from going into parking lots at night?

Yiddish has a specific phrase to describe a person who spreads gossip about things to worry about: *sorgenmeister*. Those who infect others with fear remind me of the biblical spies reporting on the dangers of venturing into the Promised Land, an apt story I also mentioned in *The Blessing of a Skinned Knee*. After traveling in the desert, Moses sent a scouting party of twelve spies to check out the territory ahead. The spies returned and reported that yes, the land was flowing with milk and honey, but it was surrounded by enemies on every side. As they told their tale, the dangers started growing. The enemies were terribly tall and terribly strong: "We looked like grasshoppers beside them!" the spies reported. And the land! "It eats the people who live there!" No wonder all the people lifted up their voices to Moses and cried: "We want to go back to Egypt!"

When you are shepherding children from childhood into adolescence you are entering a new land. You're both saying good-bye to the world of baby monitors, safety scissors, playdates, and (mostly) family board games, a world that demanded constant parental involvement. Your teen must experience much of this new world of adolescence without you, and this change of territory can make the future seem treacherous. It requires courage to move forward. Responsible parents are aware; they keep up with the facts and trends. In our complex, rapidly changing world, denial is naive and dangerous. It's appropriate to worry. But too much information about every possible danger can make it hard to be the calm, composed leader your children need as they travel toward adulthood. If you suffer from mean world syndrome, you are seeing a distorted vision of reality, and you will be too fearful to let teens make the mistakes necessary to reach maturity.

An antidote to mean world syndrome is to minimize your exposure to sensational news shows, Internet reports, and e-mail alerts. If the people in your social circle feed your fears, seek out a few level-headed parents in your neighborhood or school. Look for parents who've raised several kids into young adulthood. If you are worried about whether a particular activity is safe for a teenager, ask one of these seasoned parents. These parents have many milestones and crises behind them, and they have the advantage of perspective. Like the Jews in the wilderness, they have complained, suffered, survived—and even celebrated. Ask these experts at what age they let their child:

- Have full Web access
- Go from point A (the mall) to point B (the House of Pancakes) without calling them first
- Go to parties at the homes of families they didn't know (and did they call the parents first?)
- Stay out until midnight, or two a.m., or all night
- Go on road trips
- Attend concerts or music festivals unchaperoned

Use their answers, but don't stop there. Your teen's daily environments—home, school, activities—are natural laboratories for testing her maturity and judgment. Before you make a decision about how much freedom you will allow your child, consider the kind of evidence that turns up in these labs:

- How does your child handle technology: social networking sites, texting, IMing, safe and appropriate Internet surfing and downloading?
- How conscientious is your child about homework?
- Does your child deal with money responsibly?
- How does your child behave outside the home? Forget for a moment the way he treats his siblings and you. Is he generally polite and respectful to relatives, your adult friends, and people such as waiters, salesclerks, and cashiers?
- Is your child responsible with valuables? Does she repeatedly lose her cell phone? Does it mysteriously suffer from water damage? Does he hang up the nice blazer his grandparents bought for him? Does she replace broken guitar strings?
- How has your child handled himself in past situations where there has been temptation to make trouble?

Applying your intelligence and energy to these topics is not overparenting. Titrating the appropriate amount of freedom for your child is as important as weighing the pros and cons of the right orthodontist or SAT prep course.

THE DARK SIDE OF DEVOTION

Stepping back from our teens, locating the proper and ever-changing proportions of freedom and restriction, of wise counsel and active assistance, is never easy. But parents who have prolonged trouble detaching from their teens may need to do some soul-searching. Although overprotection can spring from misguided love, it can also occur when parents' own emotional needs cause them to seek an intensely close relationship with their teenagers. These are the parents who need to be needed. These needs are deep and multilayered, and we are not always aware of them. But the consequences are real. When teenagers sense an overprotective parent's feelings of loneliness, worthlessness, boredom, or rootlessness, they come to believe their parents *need* them to be dependent. Hidden under a parent's message of "You can't cope without me" is "I can't cope without you."

My client Lynn grew up and started a family in a small, friendly city where she worked for a small, friendly interior design firm. When Lynn's husband was offered a higher-paying job in another state, the family moved to the suburbs of a large city.

Here Lynn went into business for herself, but the work came in slowly. The clients who did come her way were wealthier, far more demanding, and as Lynn described them, "colder" than the ones in her former town. She felt lonely and isolated in her home office in the suburbs, where she didn't like to drive the long dark streets alone at night.

Meanwhile, their daughter Jenna faced her own set of challenges. She felt self-conscious and invisible as the new kid in ninth grade, and a classmate, Morgan, identified Jenna as an easy target. She conned Jenna into doing all the work on what was supposed to be a group science project; taunted her openly at school; posted pictures on Facebook of Jenna changing into her gym clothes; called Jenna and persuaded her to disclose which boy she liked and then revealed that the boy himself had been secretly listening in on a three-way call. When Jenna, sobbing, told her mother what had happened, Lynn resolved that fragile Jenna would not have to face the "mean girl" again. She determined that the only fair course of action was for the school to switch Jenna into the other ninth-grade class and suspend Morgan for her cruelty.

Now everything changed. Lynn was busy all the time. She had a whole new cast of characters in her life: the thuggish principal who considered the matter closed after Morgan offered an apology; the heartless teacher who suggested that Jenna learn some assertiveness skills; the generous family friend who offered to help Lynn initiate legal proceedings; the sympathetic private therapist. Lynn chronicled the daily maneuvers of the good guys and bad with dark humor and enthusiasm. She called her husband at work so he could help her with decisions, and she fleshed out the tales in the evening on the phone with her sister. She plotted her moves like Sun-tzu in *The Art of War*.

Jenna noticed something, too. Her mother wasn't staring at the computer all the time or pestering her about homework. She seemed happier. She wasn't on Jenna's case about getting to know new kids because she was on her *case*. She was the witness for the prosecution.

After a few weeks, the school agreed to move Jenna to a new class and sanctioned Morgan with detention and community service. It then became apparent that the social network Lynn had joined was built of straw. The house was quiet again. Then, two weeks later, Jenna came home complaining about a new outrage. A boy named Tyler had looked directly at her paper during the English exam and copied every one of her answers to the multiple-choice questions. Again Lynn was in gear, engaged and purposeful. She had a plan. Jenna's answers could be compared to Tyler's and the cheating would be made clear. Tyler was unlikely to have every answer correct, and if the pattern of his errors was identical to Jenna's, well, there would be the proof! Again she had a drama to absorb her. Did Jenna attract trouble to ease her mother's loneliness? Her problems probably had multiple causes. But the effect was obvious. Jenna's difficulties improved her mother's state of mind.

When our own need for purpose, connection, and fulfillment collides with teenagers' natural affinity for drama or dumb behavior, we have a recipe for mutual dependence. For the parents, the formula is direct: My child's problems provide me with a purpose, keep us close and connected, and prevent me from having to think about problems of my own.

In his brilliantly argued book *Addiction Proof Your Child,* Stanton Peele defines addiction as a repeated activity that makes you feel better but actually harms you, a reliance on experiences that provide "quick, sure, easy-to-obtain gratification" but "protect you from more challenging life experiences and thwart growth." Parents' addiction to teenagers makes sense because we get in the habit of fussing and fretting and pushing and adoring our children full-time, so much so that our other life skills start to wither away. But as *they* get older *we* get older, and seeing them become more independent reminds us of our mortality. It feels better to keep them dependent. This is exactly why letting go is so important.

BE A COUNSELOR, NOT A SERVANT

Our challenge as parents is to foster a loving attachment to teenagers' large spirits and ragged souls but stand slightly apart from their daily theatrics. It takes courage and finesse to detach while staying intimate. The rhythms of parent-teen relationships change every day, which means you will succeed today and screw up tomorrow. It's doubly hard because you have mighty opponents: The culture conspires against you, telling you to rush in to forestall disaster, and your child himself either cries out for help or growls for you to leave him alone when you are sure he needs guidance.

Expect to be confused. Expect your sleep to be disturbed. Try as you might, it may be hard to lovingly detach if doing so makes you feel as if you are abandoning your child or as if *you* are being abandoned. When this is the case, seek relief by stepping outside your tiny circle: Find just one sensible friend, a life coach, a therapist, a Bible study class, a course in making sushi or postmodernism or knitting, whatever works to burst the bubble of rumination and fear. Remind yourself, daily if you have to, that we serve our teens best not as active protectors or problem solvers but as tender, compassionate, composed listeners. In his 2001 book, *Glimpses of Mahayana,* the Buddhist teacher Trungpa Rinpoche cautions against what he calls "idiot compassion," in which we indulge people because we cannot bear their suffering. If we give our children what they want (a servant), instead of what they need (wise counsel), we undermine their strength and create dependency.

CHAPTER 7

The Blessing of Staying Up Late:

Making Time for Rest and Fun

A rabbi once told me about a memorable call from a congregant. One evening an eleventh grader named Connor confessed to his parents that whenever he tried to study or sleep, his heart would pound, his jaw began to ache, and he broke into a sweat. He feared he was dying. Connor's parents took him to the emergency room, where he was diagnosed with stress-induced panic attacks. Connor's mother, riding a wave of insight, called the rabbi from the ER. "You know what?" she said. "This is the first time the three of us have spent any prolonged quiet time alone together in as long as I can remember."

This story reminds me of readers' reactions to journalist Mary Kay Blakely's book *Wake Me When It's Over,* her account of falling into a coma. In her subsequent memoir, *American Mom,* Blakely writes that "hundreds of women from coast to coast thought my coma sounded like something they might want to try." One woman in Portland asked her with obvious envy, "You slept for *nine days?* How *was* that?"

Certainly going to the ER or falling into a coma is not what most of us would consider a relaxing getaway. But I frequently hear parents describe the flu or a gentle case of bronchitis as their best chance for some rest. To many parents, running a high fever feels like the only acceptable excuse for sitting out the daily whirl of orthodontist appointments, parent/teacher conferences, and late-night catch-up e-mailing.

As Connor's panic attacks show, our kids are also affected by the pressure to keep busy. School counselors are familiar with the "green beret" mentality of high school students who are certain that the only way to prove themselves is to do more than anyone else. "I can get so

115

much work done and hardly need to take a break!" they tell themselves and everyone else. These teens may insist that they're enjoying every extracurricular activity and honors class, but eventually they succumb to fatigue. They get sick. They fall asleep in class. They have car accidents. They gain or lose weight. They develop ADHD-like problems with focus and productivity. They borrow friends' stimulant medication to stay alert. They suffer from low moods and dark thoughts, and they take out their irritability on their siblings and parents.

In *The Blessing of a Skinned Knee* I talked about the time squeeze and how it affects the parents of small children. In that book, I offered a solution for young families: to alter their relationship to time, to see it not as a scarce resource but as God's bounty, a gift to be received in gratitude. More specifically, I proposed that parents take control of the family's tempo by incorporating elements of *shmirat Shabbat*—observance of the Sabbath as a day of rest—into their lives. A Shabbat dinner does more than get everyone to slow down for an hour or so. A full Shabbat dinner, complete with twinkling candles, sweet bread and wine, and a special dessert, can be a numinous experience of togetherness, rest, and renewal.

When my children were little, I loved our Shabbat dinners. They were always bountiful, unhurried meals, with guests at the table more often than not. We lit candles for those in need of healing. We linked arms and danced around the table while singing *"Shalom Aleichem"* ("Peace Be upon You"), a bouncy song welcoming the ministering angels of Shabbat to our home. We blessed the wine, the challah, and the children; during dinner we went around the table to say what we were grateful for that week. No one spoke about work, real estate, money, or problems. Instead, we often talked about the weekly Torah portion and the commentaries, especially the more rollicking details: the water splitting into twelve individual passageways when Moses and the children of Israel crossed the Red Sea, one for each tribe; the young Joseph showing off to his brothers by revealing his dream that the sun, moon, and stars bowed down to him; and the story of the "bed of Sodom," in which the evil townspeople offered wayfarers an iron bed, always the same size. If you were too tall for the bed, they cut off your legs; if you were too short, they stretched you on a rack. The stories generated rich conversations about sibling rivalry, ethics, God, fate, and life in ancient times.

A central concept in Judaism is the obligation of every single person to perform *tikkun olam,* the work of perfecting the world by redressing wrongs through acts of loving kindness and mercy. By tending to spiritual housekeeping here on the ground, we mend the rips in the cosmos. Over the course of a typical week, the fabric of a busy, robust family naturally suffers rips, too, and by talking and praying and eating together during Shabbat dinner, my family was performing holy repair work. Little holes were sewn up and mended before they became bigger. Our Friday-night dinners also connected us to our history and to the global Jewish community, to families all over the world performing the same rituals, singing the same Hebrew prayers as those sung at our table as the sun set over their homes, as our ancestors had done for centuries. These feelings opened the door to a sense of holiness and timelessness and wonder.

I assumed these cozy Shabbat dinners and their weeklong afterglow would continue through the teenage years. But then my own daughters pushed me out of the hammock. By the time Susanna and Emma were young teens, I couldn't ignore the fact that our Friday-night dinners, with their slowed-down pace, the lingering over the meal, the family discussion of Jewish stories, had become oppressive obligations.

I wasn't alone. When parents mention the upcoming Shabbat dinner, many teenagers groan. At the table, the parents float conversational gambits that promptly sink. They spot stealth texting under the table.

Their teens' reaction to a new midrash about God's magical manipulation of the waters of the Red Sea? "Oh."

To dancing around the table? "There is *no way!*"

To sitting down with family for a two-and-a-half-hour meal? "Um, sounds nice, but I'm really busy." In truth, they are.

When kids become teenagers, Shabbat becomes a challenge. They don't jump at the chance to sing *"Shalom Aleichem,"* and more and more Friday evenings are spent driving carpool to hockey games. When Shabbat dinners do take place, they become less of an opportunity to refresh and renew than an exercise in parental bitterness. *Do you think we enjoy sitting here while you have that look on your face?* parents fume to themselves as they try to maintain a conversation with their grunting child. Soon enough, the Lost Shabbat starts looking like a metaphor for the other ways your teen has moved away from you and everyone's life has sped up. Your family used to play Tickle Monster or Candyland together on weekday evenings; now that silly fun is replaced by hours of homework, two-a-day sports practices, and the ever-moving pieces of the daily logistical puzzle: How can we get Jordan back from guitar lessons in time to watch Sara at her swim meet? Even family vacations can become battlegrounds instead of rejuvenating escapes.

When you reach this point, you have a choice. You can forcefully press family time on your teenagers, or you can let go of the reins a bit. One of the many paradoxes of parenting teenagers is that if you are willing to be flexible about your family traditions, to rethink and creatively revise them, you are more likely to preserve their spirit. Sometimes this flexibility takes planning; sometimes it requires that you go with the flow. Either way, it's still your role as family leader to devise channels for uplifting downtime—for your family as a whole, for your teen, and for yourself. These strategies may not always look spiritual on the face of it, but they can be potent ways to relax, restore, and reconnect with each other.

SHABBAT WITH TEENS

If you are sighing fondly over the memory of your preschooler bringing home her first "Shabbat in a box," complete with candles, tinfoil candlesticks, and a kiddush cup decorated with tiny hearts, I commiserate. But it's not terribly difficult to engineer a teen-friendly Shabbat dinner, provided you realize that Shabbat is going to be different now. Your child won't beam with the pleasure of eating a special dinner with her entire family. Pride in knowing the prayers won't cause her to sit up taller in her seat. Your teen, once a four-year-old sparkly Shabbos Queen, may now shuffle morosely to the table, dressed in more black than Wednesday Addams. As one mother I know observed, "We went from Tot Shabbat to Goth Shabbat." But in its way, Shabbat with teens has even more potential for richness and wonder than Shabbat with preschoolers. If you can resist fussing over the details, Shabbat can become that rare commodity: a time to connect.

How do you work this miracle? Some practical strategies will help. First, decide whether it's realistic for your family to have Shabbat dinner every Friday night. In some families, the adults preserve their regular ritual even if the teens are busy elsewhere. The teens learn that Shabbat is not just the kindergarten activity they remember from years past. It's a holy ritual, and participation in it requires adult resolve and maturity. Other parents host Shabbat less frequently, but when they do, attendance is mandatory. In some families, it is enough to share a meal together on Friday night wherever they are, even if it's the House of Pies or a local Japanese restaurant. Locate your family's place on this continuum, and consider changing it when reality dictates. After the first few failed Shabbats with our teenagers, we cut the ritual in half, changed the menu, and invited any of the girls' friends who wished to participate.

I also suggest you lower your standards. If your teen shows up at the table but is huffy and glowering, just be glad he's there. As Rabbi Peretz Wolf-Prusan, senior educator of Temple Emanu-el in San Francisco, says, "If you wait for your teen to be happy about Shabbat, you are going to be waiting for a *long* time." Be patient with adolescent awkwardness in its other incarnations, too. For example, during Shabbat my family has made a tradition of lighting a candle for someone in need, saying the person's name aloud. My children and the teens who came to visit often wanted to light candles for their friends but were protective of their privacy and shy about revealing identities. We allowed them the dignity of performing this sacred act, and tried not to worry too much about who was in trouble or why.

Rabbi Wolf-Prusan points out that in San Francisco, the high schools hold dances and social events on Friday nights. He recommends parents make a two-way deal: "You show up for dinner; we'll start early enough to be done before the dance starts and we'll be happy to pick you up when it's over." If your child can't or won't join in at all, Rabbi Wolf-Prusan recommends you say, "I completely understand, but we'll miss you." This warm response not only prevents an argument, it also lets your teen know that when she decides to return to the Shabbat table, you will have a seat saved for her.

Skirt the social problem altogether by suggesting your child invite friends who won't be celebrating Shabbat with their own families for dinner and a sleepover. The guests are inevitably impressed that your kid can read the crazy squiggles of Hebrew and say exotic-sounding prayers by heart. Your child's friends may perform some impressive feats in return. My daughters recall with pride that several of their non-

Jewish friends, frequent guests at our Shabbat table, learned the words and melodies to the Hebrew prayers. Dr. Ron Wolfson, the Finger-hut Professor of Education at American Jewish University, notes that "guest teenagers are envious of this kind of time with family. Many kids have never experienced the warmth and joy of joining with their parents and siblings in a Shabbat hug, or being blessed by parents, or singing songs, or enjoying a nice meal in the dining room." Afterward, the teens can slip off to another space in the house to enjoy their own brand of togetherness.

My favorite part of Shabbat with teens is the traditional blessing of the children. You whisper a prayer in the child's ear while gently holding his head. The thirty seconds it takes to say the blessing are intimate, tender, and wildly unlike everyday teen-parent interactions. I've never seen a teen resist it. The prayer itself is beautiful, and particularly touching when said over a teen who is in an "undivine" state of development:

May the Lord make you like [if the child is a girl] *Sarah, Rebecca, Rachel, and Leah.* For boys, you say, *"like Ephraim and Menasseh."*
May the Lord bless you and watch over you.
May the Lord cause the Divine face to shine upon you and be gracious to you.
May the Lord lift up the Divine face toward you and bring you peace.
Amen.

EXTENDING SHABBAT THROUGH THE WEEK

A ritual at the end of Shabbat dinner invites its mystical feeling to linger throughout the week. I'm speaking of *havadalah,* a short ceremony that uses all five senses to seal in the memory of Shabbat. After lighting a braided, multiwicked candle, diners pass around the *bessamim,* a delicate silver container, and smell the spices inside. They drink wine from the kiddush cup and dot or wipe it on their eyelids to continue Shabbat's clarity of vision long after the dinner is over.

The metaphor is beautiful, but its application is tricky. How do you preserve the slowed-down, intimate feeling of the Sabbath when life returns to its usual hyperscheduled state? I suggest looking for small opportunities to connect with teens. Don't smother them with attention—they will only squirm away—but feel free to try a more subtle approach, like taking them out for a meal. Your teenagers may be criti-

cal of your cooking, or they may develop annoying dietary requirements ("I told you no gluten!"), but they will rarely turn down a
restaurant meal when someone else is paying. An added bonus is that
teens are cheap dates. For the price of a salad, a pizza, and a drink, you
can share a relaxing half hour during which a few pleasantries may be
exchanged.

There will be times when your teen is eager to reach out and connect
with you. These mystical moments can come disguised as the urgent
command: "Mom! Mom! You *have* to watch this video of a bulldog riding a skateboard!" Or maybe it's a willingness to make small talk while
you're driving home from baseball practice. In these cases, drop everything to watch the skateboarding bulldog. Take the long way home
from the field to keep your teen talking. If your teen decides to open his
heart to you while you're doing chores, don't scare him away by making a big production of sitting him down, shutting the door, and grilling
him with annoying questions. But do listen to every word, and unfold
and refold the laundry as many times as it takes your teen to tell you
he's worried about starting ninth grade because he's so short, or that she
thinks she's the only girl in tenth grade who has never made out with a
boy, or that she doesn't know what to say to her best friend whose parents are getting a divorce.

FAMILY FUN: ARE WE THERE YET?

Another way to create opportunities for family rest and togetherness is
to revisit old traditions or invent some new ones. When your children
were small there were traditions particular to your family that shaped
some of your favorite moments. They may have been birthday or holiday celebrations, worship services, or annual vacations. These occasions
either revived your own best experiences from childhood or created
new ones. They etched themselves in your memory through your
senses—the glittering holiday lights; the foods that tasted particularly
delicious because you made them only on birthdays; the fresh, spicy
smell of cedar in the mountainside cabin you rented yearly.

And now? Maybe your family traditions are still securely in place.
Maybe your fifteen-year-old can't wait for the holidays to roll around.
Maybe your high school junior is eagerly planning this year's annual

family trip to the amusement park. But more often, their attitudes have changed.

Nevertheless, it is possible to maintain (or resurrect) family traditions and still have fun. Family fun with teenagers takes more effort than it did when your children were little. You will need to consciously protect the kind of rituals that your teenagers seem to barely tolerate but may secretly prize. What sorts of traditions do teens prefer? Anything that doesn't require smiling, nice clothes, or small, enclosed places with adults who ask hated questions like "Where are you thinking of applying to college? Got a girlfriend yet?" Conduct a few experiments in ignoring their reticence. One trick is to ask teens if they will bake some cookies or a cake with you for the holidays. They may act like they are doing you a favor by agreeing to help, but often they'll get into the spirit of things once you pull out the flour and chocolate chips. Or ask them to help you decorate the house for a big party. (In the spirit of Goth Shabbat, be prepared for some edgy choices.)

At the same time, know when to bend traditions that cause too much friction. When our girls were small, Rosh Hashanah was a favorite religious holiday. Along with the rest of our congregation, we observed the solemn and inspiring rite of *tashlich* at the beach. After services, everyone changed from their more formal temple clothes into jeans and baseball caps. We performed the ritual of casting our sins (written on a piece of paper and torn into pieces or symbolized by bread crumbs) into the ocean to symbolically wipe the slate clean of past transgressions and prepare for happiness and goodness in the year ahead. The rabbi or cantor played the guitar as the small children played in the sand and at the water's edge. It was sweet. Strung along the beach from Venice to Malibu were scores of other congregations all casting, praying, singing, and then picnicking.

One year when our children were teenagers, they announced that they didn't want to go to the beach for *tashlich*. No, they wanted to go to the L.A. River. The unromantic river, with polluted water and steep concrete banks, in an urban neighborhood.

We agreed. Instead of a picnic we took our dogs, a friend from the block, the girls' uncle and cousins, and their dog. No one but our group was at the river. The terrier rolled in horse manure, the water spaniel surfed, and the retriever tried to retrieve the sins after we threw them in the water.

Everyone loved it. Even though our spot on the river was situated near a highly trafficked boulevard, there were huge, swaying willows, sycamore trees, and cattails along the banks. We wrote our sins down, solemnly, while sitting on the bare concrete, and then watched them drift down the river around the bend and out of sight—a symbolism that doesn't work when you throw bits of paper into the ocean and watch them drift back to shore. When the ceremony was over we went to a do-it-yourself dog wash down the street to wash and brush and dry the dogs, and everyone got back in the car invigorated, cleansed of mud and sins. Yes, the adults missed both the beach and the big throng of our large congregation, and it took some mental adjustment to accept the necessity of a visit to a dog wash on a holy day. But in Judaism, we are all made in God's image. One way to exhibit reverence for God is to accommodate his holy stand-ins—in this case, our teenagers. Just as with the Sabbath, we kept the intent but bent the particulars.

The same attitude works for vacations. Some destinations don't easily lend themselves to family fun with teens: amusement parks (even though they enjoy going with their friends); family resorts where most of the families have little kids or your teen doesn't know anyone other than you; a long road trip with five people in a five-seater car; any place where Americans may get *touristas* if they eat any nonhotel food. If a trip like one of these has been a tradition for your family, consider a new destination. Ask friends with teenage children what has worked for them.

Tailor your trip to a place that reflects your teen's interests. One summer, our family took a trip to Iceland because Emma loved Scandinavian pop music and Susanna, the geology student, could study the black lava fields and volcanoes. My husband and I cherished the opportunity to bathe in warm-water blue lagoons. The whole family looked forward to walking with crampons on the glaciers. It took months of planning and saving, but as a once-in-a-lifetime event it was a portal to family connection and unforgettable memories. The summer after the Iceland trip, the economy collapsed—and we had a great time at a rented cabin on a pond in New Hampshire where the girls had friends from home staying nearby. We hiked and kayaked and swam in the day. Some evenings we played word games, others they spent with their friends.

If you're taking the kind of vacation that can inexpensively accommodate an extra guest, consider bringing a friend along for your teen. A friend on a trip has many advantages. He or she may help absorb the stickiness of so much family togetherness, and you aren't saddled with the burden of providing constant entertainment for your teen. You can bring friends, too. That way, parents and teens can divide up when everyone needs a break.

IN PRAISE OF WASTED TIME

Creating new rituals for your family takes some dexterity, but it's also fun. Plus, you are still in control; you take your teen's interests and temperament into account, but you're the one who sets the parameters. Your next task is more difficult. You must learn to respect your teenager's own strategies for relaxing without you.

Your teen may enjoy the parent-approved methods for winding down: exercise, reading, and hobbies. Or he may lean toward the less wholesome teen-approved methods of partying and pushing the boundaries of the law. We'll talk about those later in the book. Here, I want to endorse a different set of relaxation strategies, ones that are not as potentially destructive as drugs or drinking or other foolhardy or defiant acts but that nevertheless put parents on edge. I'm talking about those blatant time-wasters with little obvious redeeming value: socializing and surfing online, immature goofing around with friends, and low-culture pleasures like trashy TV.

Do Not Fear the Internet

Some parents adopt suspicion as their default stance toward technology, especially the Internet. They justify a clamp-down on computer use by saying, "I just want to make sure she's safe" or "I need to be sure she's using the computer for homework, not just fooling around." But cyberlife is the new village green or corner stoop—a place for teens to wind down, express their individuality, and connect with friends away from nosy parents. The Web provides rich opportunities for them to do these things.

How does a parent wisely guide their teen's Internet use? Not with keystroke capture or screenshot programs, which allow the parent to monitor every single thing a child does online. Parents' fear of the Web is often fueled by news reports about cyberpredators who use the Internet to lure teens out of their homes and into harm's way. The cable news networks and shows like the infamous *To Catch a Predator* attract viewers by playing on our horrified reaction to these scary strangers. But is the fear of cyberpredators based in reality? In a 2009 article that appeared in the journal *American Psychologist,* Janis Wolak and a team of coresearchers concluded that many parental fears about online activity are unjustified. Between 1993 and 2005, a time when the Internet became widely available to teens, sexual assaults on teenagers actually fell by fifty-two percent. Nor is it particularly risky for teens to interact online with friends of friends or even strangers who share their interests. Wolak points out that risky behavior is not chatting with people you haven't met face-to-face (which many teens do all the time) but giving out names, phone numbers, or pictures, or talking to strangers about sex.

The real dangers for children in cyberspace are less dramatic than kidnapping or molestation, but they are still reason for concern. These include the "Web potato" effect of eye strain and reduced physical vigor, the emotional disturbance of exposure to ugly or frightening images and reputation damage. Teens can be naive about the long-lasting effects of posting compromising photos of their friends or themselves, and because cybercommunication does not take place face-to-face, they can be callous about hurting other people's feelings with online gossip. Treat your teen's forays into the cyberworld as you would similar experiences in the physical world, by using the "natural laboratory" concept I described earlier in this book. Titrate her online freedom in doses appropriate to her good judgment in the other testing grounds of her life. You tailor a teen's curfew to her age and responsibility; it is perfectly appropriate to do the same with computers by keeping hers in a common room of the house, using a filter, and withholding access to an internet-enabled cell phone until your teen has demonstrated that she is mature enough to roam freely. When assessing your teen's readiness for the online world, consider these questions:

• Does she meet her homework and test preparation obligations independently, without lots of nagging?

- Is she responsible for her health, hygiene, and chores?
- Do her teachers give you positive reports?
- Is she generally respectful to adults and compassionate toward her peers?
- Does she neglect activities that are generally considered to be useful to the well-rounded human being, for example, reading anything at all for pleasure, spending time outdoors, and visiting with friends in person?

In addition to your child's general level of maturity, think about her temperament. Is she sensitive? How would your thirteen-year-old react to a graphic pornographic image or to footage of a hostage beheading? Everything is accessible on the Web. Families should discuss their values, come to some common conclusions about what is allowed, and then agree on a contract for Web use.

Plan to revisit your contract frequently. Technology and its uses change rapidly—schools modify their Internet policies every year—and our kids grow so quickly that what is safe and sound in March may be unfairly restrictive over the summer. And uphold your end of the bargain. Don't pretend to grant your teen unlimited cyber privacy and then spy on her browsing history or Facebook page when she's at school.

Provide Space for Immaturity

As much as teens wish to have the independence of adults, they enjoy being juvenile. Like little kids, they love to make up games. They might pass people on the street and whisper to each other, "Your team," if the person is unattractive or odd or "My team" if they are cute or "hot." At a music festival or theme park or any large gathering of youth they might go "fishing" by calling out a name chosen at random: "Jake!" or "Miles!" or "Ashley!" or "Samantha!"—until someone turns around blinking in puzzlement. They love sexual innuendo. One currently popular joke involves saying "twess," which is short for "That's what she said," after any suggestive phrase. On the Natural History Museum tour the docent says, "This is an unusually large spear." Teen A whispers to Teen B: "Twess." Or during a history test one teen mutters, "This is too hard!" And the friend shoots back, "Twess." Of course, they revel in bathroom humor. One mother found her son and his friends laughing over a website devoted to the world's largest poops.

Silly? Immature? You bet, and that's why it is such an effective way to relax. It's a break from the hard work of preparing for the grown-up world. Don't panic that teens' juvenile behavior is a character flaw or that they are losing precious time that could be spent improving themselves. You don't have to participate in the silliness with them, but make sure you are not reflexively obstructing their opportunities to indulge with friends. Allowing them time to mess around together, to waste aeons of time at music festivals, the mall, or in your basement, is both respectful and fair.

Demonstrate Respect for Junk Pleasures

I often ask audiences of parents to call out the activities they grudgingly allow their children:

"Watch?"
"Family Guy!"
"Eat?"
"Oreos!"
"Do?"
"Play Grand Theft Auto!"
"Listen to?"
"Kanye! System of a Down!"

Then I say, "If you are going to let them do it, accept it and appreciate it."

Ask about their favorite YouTube video or episode of a shockingly crass reality show. Maintain a friendly, respectful tone. Think of the encounter as cultural anthropology, or undercover reporting. Resist the urge to see this as a teachable moment, one that will lift them out of their immaturity. You may be tempted to think, *I'll let them watch* America's Next Top Model *but I'll take the opportunity to do a little media literacy at the same time.* Then you might say, "Did you know that if she were alive, Barbie would be a woman standing seven feet tall with a waistline of eighteen inches and a bustline of forty? In fact, she would need to walk on all fours just to support her bizarre proportions!" Or, during

Gay, Straight, or Taken, you provide a little sex ed: "Did you know that the average teen will view nearly fourteen thousand sexual references per year in the media but that only one percent of those will talk about birth control and the risk of pregnancy or STDs?"

You can make this sort of consciousness-raising speech every now and then, but most of the time zip your lip. If you allow teens to watch a show, let them watch it in peace. From time to time, sit down and watch the show together. Grab a handful of the Oreos that are spilled out on the table and enjoy them. Doing so is not an indulgence; it's an affirmation of their taste.

NIGHT: TIME TO STAY UP LATE OR TIME TO SLEEP?

Teenagers love to stay up late. They enjoy the freedom, independence, and privacy of being awake when everyone else is asleep. In the quiet and dark they may use less electricity in a literal sense, but there is a special crackle of mental energy. It's like being in the forest of the mind. Teens enjoy using nighttime to unwind, to develop their sense of self and identity. They connect with one another via texts or online, or on weekends they get together at one another's houses, watching movies and talking until the early-morning hours.

These late hours, so bewildering to tired parents, come to teens courtesy of their developing circadian rhythms. These biological clocks encourage the release of hormones that wake young children and adults up in the morning light and prepare us for sleep as night falls. In adolescence, however, circadian rhythms shift, so that it can be difficult for teens to fall asleep in the evening; they are often naturally alert and wakeful well past midnight. Then, ideally, they zonk out until midmorning. When teens take advantage of weekends to sleep even later, until lunchtime or early afternoon, they are not being lazy. They are recovering from the jetlag effect produced by waking up on an adult schedule during the school week. To them, living according to school hours is like taking the red-eye from Los Angeles to New York every morning.

The natural tendency of teens to stay up late is exaggerated by their structured, enriched schedules. The homework load at many schools demands several hours of work each night, and if teens are at drama rehearsal or tennis practice until six, seven, or eight o'clock, they can't even begin that homework until well past dinner. And because they are deprived of "free range" time during the day and evening, they may carve out time late into the night to wind down outside the watchful eye of adults. When parents constantly monitor what their child eats, drinks, who he hangs out with, and how and when he does his homework, they give him another reason to stay up late. It's his shot at independence.

Before you decide that your teen's habit of staying up late is a problem, make sure you're not projecting panic about your own sleep debt onto your teen. Some teens can shrug off a little sleeplessness during weekdays without much ill effect. They don't fear sleep loss the way adults do, probably because they can catch up on sleep on the weekends. And unlike us, their sleeplessness isn't associated with unpleasant worries about credit card bills and work pressures. Think of a teen's sleep schedule as practice for college, where many students keep a European schedule: staying up late, getting up for class, and taking a siesta in the afternoon.

For some teens, however, even small amounts of sleep loss result in illness and irritability. Serious, persistent sleeplessness will impair nearly everyone. Just as young children who don't get enough outdoor playtime are sometimes mislabeled as having attention deficits, teens who don't get enough sleep may look depressed, learning impaired, or even bipolar. If your teen is consistently cranky, unmotivated, inattentive, or if he requires a Sonic Boom alarm clock to wake up in the morning and then consistently nods off in class (a key indicator of sleep deprivation), he may need more sleep.

Of course, you can't force your teen to sleep. But you can help set a scene that encourages slumber. Make sure your teen knows the basics of sleep hygiene: Is he drinking caffeine after four p.m.? Staying up very, very late on Friday and Saturday and then trying to get to sleep early on Sunday evening? Using his bed for studying or watching television? And the big one: allowing distractions to keep him awake? Technology, the very thing that allows him to unwind, is also a deterrent to reasonable amounts of sleep. Allow your teen time every night to enjoy technology, but set a cutoff point. I often required my daughters to place their laptops and cell phones outside their bedrooms after ten-thirty at night;

I viewed it as the cyber equivalent of telling party guests that it's time to go home.

What if your teen's homework or activity schedule is the cause of sleep loss? Some teens experiment with doing too much, and it does not do permanent harm if they suffer the natural consequences of fatigue and exhaustion for a short period of time. It can be a helpful lesson they carry into adult life. But teens also lack the perspective of adults, and because they are locked inside a competitive culture, they may not see an alternative to consistent overscheduling. They may not even realize that they are suffering. In these cases, you may need to require them to drop some extracurriculars or even classes in school that are overly taxing because of their difficulty or the workload required. In a world where teens are measured by how many AP classes they can pack into a school day, this can be hard for parents to do. It feels truly dangerous. Say to yourself, *She is being too good, too productive, too ambitious, and I see it is hurting her spirit and her well-being.* And then say to your eleventh grader, "I am stepping in here because I see how stressed you are even if you don't see it yourself. I'm strongly recommending that you take a break from the teen help line this month." Or, "It is not advisable for you to take two AP classes *and* run on the varsity cross-country team next semester even though I know you really want to."

PARENTS, FIND TIME FOR FLOW

Raising teenagers is an endurance race, not a sprint. If you want the strength to guide your child through the process of separation from you, you'll need to have regular time when you are separate from them. You must be sure to tend to yourself: to enjoy the company of good friends; to read things that are not report cards, catalogs, or college brochures; to listen to things that are not your teenager's voice; to taste things that are new and delicious; to shift into a slower, more soothing rhythm.

I also suggest that you pursue activities that, like Shabbat dinner, change your relationship to time, that absorb you so fully you don't notice the minutes or hours passing. This feeling of being lost in time is called *flow*. Psychologist Mihaly Csikszentmihalyi, currently of the Drucker Institute at Claremont Graduate University, developed the concept. He has devoted his life's work to the study of what makes people happy and has determined that engaging in activities that put you in a flow state is crucial to feeling fulfilled.

What causes us to enter a state of flow? For some people it is mastering a new sport or learning to play poker, for others it is group prayer, musical improvisation, making art, trying a challenging new recipe, or diving into playful or exciting sex (not check-off-the-to-do-list sex). To get into a state of flow, you must be doing one thing with intense focus, not a variety of things with divided attention. One of my own favorite gateways to flow is snorkeling, an activity guaranteed to take me out of time and space and everyday worries. There are no sounds. You can't talk to people, only point. You see nothing but colors, light, and movement while your body gently sways in the waves. Some senses are restricted and others are saturated, an unusual situation that brings your attention into complete focus. But like most people, I don't live near the beach in Hawaii, so I also hike, garden, and bake.

Look around for your own preferred means of changing the psychic channel. When you do something so absorbing that it causes a state of flow, you are gathering holy sparks, making good use of the universe's offerings. You exit the state refreshed for life with your teens. When Shabbat dinner comes around, you will have something more interesting to talk about than your child's upcoming English paper.

SANCTUARY

In addition to making time for rest, parents need to establish a private, nurturing space that is off-limits to teens. I recently had the following conversation with Allie, a tall, pretty fourteen-year-old with a twinkle in her eye. Her mother, Susan, had brought Allie in to see if I could break her of the habit of ignoring certain house rules.

"Your mom seems pretty upset. What do you think gets her going like that?"
I began.
"I go into her closet and take her clothes."
"What happens next?"
"I do it again."
"Right away?"
"Yup."

"Why? What's the draw?"

"I like her clothes so much better than mine."

Obviously, Allie's mother was not annoyed enough to actually do something about the problem, such as making borrowing privileges contingent on cooperation. I knew from talking to Susan that she appreciated how beautiful her daughter looked in these garments, which were much more expensive than anything she could justify buying for a teenager. Allie picked up on the double message, so she continued to raid the closet. But how will this mother feel if her daughter starts taking her jewelry or her car without asking?

We must draw bright lines between our world and theirs. One line is drawn at your bedroom. Make it into a sanctuary—an attractive, quiet shelter for adults. Explain to your children that your bedroom is a private, adult space. Keep the door closed and require that your teens knock and receive permission before entering. Make and enforce rules about borrowing your clothes, your makeup, or using your bathroom.

The concept of sanctuary extends beyond your material items and your private space. It includes your emotions and thought processes. You have the right to be in a bad temper, and you don't need to have a good reason. Nor are you required to tell your teenagers the motives behind every decision. They do not need to know the family income, why you don't see a particular friend anymore, your sexual history, or any other private information you don't wish to disclose. Sanctuary even extends to the kinds of things you may normally long for, like the closeness of having them sit on your lap. A part of you says, *Incredible! A teenager wants to sit on my lap! I'm so thrilled. It's like when she was a little baby.* But you might not be in the mood for it at that particular moment, and that's your right. You can say, "Not right this minute but come back later when I've had a chance to relax for a bit." Or if your home is the hangout of choice, you can put limits on the volume of visitors even as you love that they feel comfortable and happy in your company. If you deprive yourself of space and privacy, if you become the family martyr with no boundaries protecting you, you are more likely to react to your teenager's bad moods with anger or despair or resentment. Maintaining sanctuary is preventive spiritual nourishment.

TEENAGERS AS INSPIRATION

When your children were little, it was easy to see the world through their eyes. When you weren't irritated because they were late getting dressed and the van was coming up the driveway to pick them up for carpool, you could get on their wavelength, slow down and appreciate their fluid sense of time. You, too, could put aside the tasks at hand to appreciate the allure of a handful of smooth stones or their enchantment with a soap bubble.

Teenagers do not provide a similar gateway to a peaceful suspension of time. But the goal of holy rest is not just relaxation but refreshment, and here teens can be an inspiration. Teens can remind us of what we have lost through fearfulness, exhaustion, withdrawal, and tentativeness. Where adults are polite and numb, teens are rude and vibrant. They know the pleasure of taking a really long hot shower, wearing clothing that expresses their unique vision of beauty, sleeping for as long as they need to, enjoying food and drink with gusto, slacking off, skin-to-skin contact, a big dramatic fight with a good friend and the pleasure of making up afterward, and the violent, tender, personal pleasure of music. They will not extend an invitation for you to join in whatever captivates them, and often you wouldn't want to anyway. But if you respectfully observe their expertise in wholehearted indulgence, you may find yourself with a fresh supply of energy.

CHAPTER 8

The Blessing of Breaking the Rules:

Real Life as Ethics Lab

You want your teen to know right from wrong, to understand the standards laid down by society and your family, and also to make decisions that flow from both self-respect and respect for others. But this is complicated stuff, and teens are, by nature, experiential learners. There's no real understanding of biology without the lab, and there's no real transmission of values without trial and error. So you can talk to your teen about your family's values. You can send him to Sunday school and personal growth summer camp. He can participate in character education classes, role-playing scenarios about plagiarism and bullying, prejudice, integrity, and self-respect. But like the small child who just *has* to test the theory about tongues and frozen pipes, the healthy teen needs to test the true shape and form of the adult's code of ethics. Adults say certain acts and attitudes are wrong, but teens need to explore the boundaries of these statements: When, where, how, with whom? Do we really mean what we say? What are the exceptions?

What if you're a kid without a decent allowance and you steal something from a store? What if you work in that store? Are the consequences more or less severe?

What happens when you are very clever and write the answers for the history test on the back of a water bottle label and glue it back on?

What if you shield a friend who is taking money from the other kids' backpacks but don't take any yourself?

What if you're supposed to dog-sit for the neighbors and you throw a big party in their basement?

If you sell weed behind the strip mall?

135

If you help out a friend by lending him your homework?

Many parents find these situations frightening, but this is what normal, healthy ethical fieldwork looks like. When they encounter the answers to these questions, teens acquire a deep, internally learned sense of society's behavioral code. At some point, every teen will lie and cover it up, sneak around, cheat on a test, shoplift, break a few rules, or break a few laws. The vast majority of them are not heading for a life behind bars. They're just doing little and big experiments. It's vital for them to perform these experiments now, while they are still under your roof, rather than later, when they are subject to harsher consequences in adulthood. Don't panic at the first sign of ethical immaturity. If you do, you won't have the poise and strength to play the role of your child's moral steward, to teach the lessons that their experiments are designed to reveal.

HOW PARENTS GET IN THE WAY

When your teen transgresses, the very first item on your parental checklist is to stop and ask yourself whether you are unwittingly aiding and abetting the activity. Like animal snares that hunters camouflage with leaves and vines, parental ethics traps are masked by their innocent appearance.

The Loyalty Trap

Overly loyal parents blame their teen's unethical actions on extenuating circumstances. Cheating is blamed on unskilled teachers or unfair coaches; bullying is caused by unsavory peers; rule-breaking is caused by rigid institutional rules or ignorance of the law. A school administrator once came up to me after my talk at a conference and wryly said: "When I was a kid, if you came home and complained that the teacher put a gun to your head, your mom asked, 'What did you do to deserve it?'" Today the pendulum has swung so far in the other direction that if a student breaks school rules, parents rush in, high upon horses, swords drawn, to avenge wrongs done to their children, rather than *by* them.

When you feel the urge to protect and defend your teen from the consequences of his behavior, redefine loyalty. When you side with your child's rationalizations or excuses, or when you act as if the world is too rough a place for your teen to manage without parental defenders, you are being loyal . . . to your child's past as a baby. But when you allow your child to experience the pain that follows his wrong actions and to learn from that pain, you demonstrate deep loyalty to your child's future as an independent, accountable adult.

The Trap of Kindly Objectivity

Sometimes parents sound more like detached therapists than stewards of their child's ethical development. *Because of my husband's transfers, we've moved four times since Josh was in fourth grade, so Josh had to learn to use whatever social calling card fit the new time and place. My sense is that he saw selling Ecstasy on the school bus as a quick and effective way to get to know people in a huge, bewildering middle school. When you look at Josh's actions from his perspective, it's easy to understand his mistake.*

It's good to be fair, to give the benefit of the doubt, but go too far and you will obscure the true meaning and impact of poor choices. When you rationalize your child's actions, you are not teaching him to take care of himself. You are teaching him to self-handicap, to believe he is too simpleminded, lacking in self-control, or impaired to learn how to live life without breaking rules and laws.

The Entertainment Trap

Are you entertained by your child's transgressions? Do their high jinks invite you into a world you never visited as a teen or even bring back enjoyable memories? *(Ah, when we were seniors, we wrote the numbers of our graduation year in weed killer on the football field.)* One father smiled as he told me: "I've been a member of NORML since I was in college, so smoking pot with Oliver [his seventeen-year-old son] just seems 'normal.'"

If you are too tickled by your child's behavior, too confident that his current actions will make for a cute story when he's forty, your reaction will be lacking an appropriate sense of parental gravitas. You won't be able to say what your child needs to hear, which is some version of "Are you nuts?" Even if you do voice disapproval to your child for his behavior, the light in your eyes will give you away.

The Scapegoating Trap

Without realizing it, some troubled families use their teen as a convenient scapegoat. In family therapy, the term "identified patient" (IP) refers to a family member who is holding the symptoms for the group. The IP acts depressed or antisocial in reaction to, or as a way to cover for, family problems. These may include substantial problems, like a parent's addiction, infidelity, or abuse; less dramatic but chronic problems like marital disappointment; and unwritten "rules," like "No one ever speaks about Dad's bad temper." The IP, like all scapegoats, has another function as well. He bonds the rest of the family together by providing endless subject matter for conversation and a sense of solidarity. *We got another call from the school today. Wait until you hear what Max and his little buddies tried to pull off this time.* When the therapist treats the symptoms of the IP and he gets better, new symptoms predictably pop up in another family member. Until the root cause of the family problem is uncovered, the symptoms continue to make their rounds.

Casting blame on an IP can be particularly tempting for newly blended families in which the members don't yet have their sea legs: *That boy is lazy, sneaky, ungrateful, and irresponsible. And you always defend him. Always. If it wasn't for him we would all be getting along gloriously.* Well, maybe, but in reality weaving a new family together is a big, bulky project.

The Fatigue Trap

Supervising and guiding teenagers is a shocking amount of work. It's as grueling as chasing after a toddler all day but lacks the immediate rewards of cuddling an affectionate, contented, enchanting child. Sometimes parents minimize their teenager's negative behavior so they can avoid the difficult slog of confronting their teen, creating consequences, and enforcing those consequences day after day after day. If you spend too much time creating busywork for yourself, surfing the Web, or gossiping with your friends or the teachers *about* your child instead of getting in his face, you are a parent slacker. This is understandable. It's easier to go online and avoid conflict than to have a fight. You may even tell yourself that you are not angry. But avoiding conflict is tiring, and in the end it produces an ethically slippery child.

• • •

Have you fallen into one of these traps? More than one? Don't waste time beating yourself up over whatever "failing" you might have. We've all got them. Move on to the next step, which is a shift in strategy. If you're *too* loyal, forgiving, and tickled by your teen's bad behavior, you are, as they say in the twelve-step programs, "enabling" it. If you suspect that your teen may be the identified patient—the canary in the coal mine alerting the family to a need for openness, for breathable air—talk to a therapist for guidance. If you are too tired to face your child, you'll need to stop, size up your resources, and look for ways to refuel and re-arm. Then you'll have the energy for the next step, which is preparing yourself to issue consequences for your teen's transgressions.

CONQUER YOUR FEAR OF CONSEQUENCES

Teens who perform ethical fieldwork won't learn the contours of society's rules unless their poor decisions come with penalties. When your child behaves badly, you must impose consequences.

Plenty of parents feel squeamish or confused about consequences, especially if their own parents' mode of discipline felt more like retribution than an effective lesson:

You smoked a cigarette? Here, let's see how you feel when you have to smoke a whole pack!

Or if you felt they condemned or diminished *you* rather than your behavior:

Go to your room and stay there. You disgust me.

Or if you ended up feeling ashamed rather than encouraged when there were no consequences at all:

Saw your report card. No surprises there.

But penalties for misdeeds and mistakes, appropriately administered, are a rich teaching tool. They communicate: "Uh-oh. You didn't think this through. Your poor choice cost us money, or damaged my confidence in your word, or tarnished our good family name in the community, or diminished my ability to be free of worry or consternation. For this you must make amends."

Consequences teach about direction: *not here, not now, not that way; but here, now, this way.* How can parents preserve a loving connection and their teenager's lively spirit while teaching a lesson? The rabbis offer guidance.

TESHUVAH

The Jewish word for repentance is *teshuvah*, which means "return," and it carries with it the idea that the sinner is one who has simply lost his way or gotten off track. And the rabbis believe that the best way to undo damage, to extract a worthy lesson from a mistake, is for the sinner to ride back into the good graces of the community in whatever vehicle he rode out on. The great modern Jewish ethicist Rabbi Joseph Telushkin quotes the wisdom of the thirteenth-century rabbi Jonah Girondi:

The repentant sinner should strive to do good with the same faculties with which he sinned . . . with whatever part of the body he sinned, he should now engage in good deeds. If his feet have run to sin, let them now run to the performance of the good. If his mouth had spoken falsehood, let it now be open to wisdom. Violent hands should now be open to charity . . . the troublemaker should now become a peacemaker.

When you teach your child how to do *teshuvah*, you take him back to the problem he caused so that he can return what has been lost. Natural consequences will take effect (drive too fast, get a speeding ticket; drive too fast again, have your license suspended), but *teshuvah* also goes beyond them. *Teshuvah* transforms the misdeed into self-knowledge and strength. The rabbis say that the repentant sinner stands at a place closer to God than he who has never sinned. The sinner knows what tempts him and what *not* to do next time. He has matured; he knows regret.

Decide on proper *teshuvah* for your teen's misbehavior based on what needs to be returned to the family or community: for example, trust, time, or goods. Doing *teshuvah* can be simple:

Because you didn't go to your dentist appointment when you said you would, you'll have to call Dr. Schmidt, apologize, and reschedule on your own.

Not home by curfew? Next weekend you'll have to stay home so we'll know exactly where you are and won't have to worry.

You and your friends left a big mess in the den. I want you to clean it up— and reserve Sunday to help me clean out the attic.

In the case of serious ethical breaches, *teshuvah* might require more effort:

We are very upset and disappointed that you threw a party in our house while we were out of town. You'll have to clean up the mess and pay for the damage out of your own money. We also want you to call the parents of your friends who came to the party and apologize for putting their children in jeopardy.

When another adult or institution administers consequences for your child's behavior, it's your job to endorse them, even if the results are painful. You'll also need to add your own layer of *teshuvah*:

Mr. Stanley says he is going to give you an F in his class because you cheated on the test. So that takes care of the consequence from the school. But in order to right this wrong, we want you to volunteer in the afterschool tutoring program twice a week for a month.

Drew, we will come with you to court and stand by your side while you hear what the judge has to say about the shoplifting. But no matter what happens in court, we want you to repair the damage to our family name. You'll have to donate twenty hours of community service cleaning up the green areas around the mall.

Rabbi Sidney Schwartz, founder of the Washington Institute of Jewish Leadership and Values, an organization devoted to inspiring young people to do good works, describes teenagers as having a "thick crust of self-centeredness covering a deep well of idealism." Although teenagers see themselves as the center of the universe, they are passionate and full of conviction. Doing *teshuvah* allows them to harness these attributes. By "doing time" for a misdeed, teens stretch and develop greater ethical maturity.

Say Less Than Comes to Mind

Helping a teen do *teshuvah* doesn't require much talking. In *The Blessing of a Skinned Knee*, I described the importance of issuing a rebuke—a gentle, spoken reprimand—and explaining misbehavior to a young child. When rebuked, little children will often cry or look abashed; even if they defend themselves or blame their sister, you can sense that your words have been absorbed. Teens, however, will be dismissive of your rebuke. Worse, they may issue a deft counterargument:

How can it be wrong to take one tiny bottle of body spray from the Gap?

They overcharge so much there, it's like they're *robbing* me *every time I buy a T-shirt! I was just evening things up.*

It's fifty-five. Fifty-five miles an hour, Dad! That's insane. If you go fifty-five everyone passes you even in the right lane. And get this, there was no one *in front of me. Not one car. And I get a ticket. This so sucks.*

I've never done anything like this before, so I don't understand why you are making such a big deal out of it. Doesn't my past record of good behavior stand for anything? I've just been too good; that's the problem. Now if I do one *thing wrong it's the end of the world.*

When you hear this kind of response, getting sucked into legalisms is almost irresistible. Your child starts a sentence with the word "but," and you're off to the courtroom, defending your stance, never to find your way back to the real issue ("But Mom, *you* said that . . ."). Or you up the ante, simply to make sure your message has gotten through. One mother I was working with got so frustrated that she went over the edge, telling her son: "I hope you're happy that you've ruined my life." She did not intend to humiliate her son, although that was the effect. She was just frustrated that he didn't seem to listen or care.

Make sure that you clearly state the problem when you are issuing consequences, but skip the lectures. Teens tune you out after the first two sentences anyway. They are people of action, and to communicate effectively with them you must be a parent of action. Define the problem simply and clearly, ignore their protests and jabs, and then explain the *teshuvah,* the amends, your teen is required to perform.

Follow Through

Doing *teshuvah* requires sacrifice all around. Your teenager has to give something up (freedom, fun, money, or time), and so do you. You have to devote yourself to monitoring the consequences you've chosen. If your teen is grounded, you are, too. If your teen is doing *teshuvah* by tutoring in the afternoons, you might have to drive him home. But without follow-through, *teshuvah* becomes nothing more than a well-intentioned but hollow mission statement. So before you start issuing consequences, check for any personal vulnerability in this domain:

• Are you so busy, forgetful, or disorganized that you ignore the plan you set out for making amends? (If so, your child will just hear your rebuke as the usual buzz, an annoying noise that will stop eventually if he just ignores it.)

- Are you hot-headed, meting out harsh consequences in anger and retracting them later? Do you feel so much emotional satisfaction from getting angry that your tirade alone feels like sufficient discipline? (It isn't. Your child will just write it off as a "parent tantrum.")
- Do you gather thorns, bringing up all your child's past crimes or saying "you always" or "you never"? (This will demoralize your child rather than encourage him to improve.)
- Do you make a punishment "gesture," and then grow so fearful of breaking the delicate thread of connection with your teenager that you find yourself taking him out for ice cream? Do you let your child beg, plead, sweet-talk, or distract you out of punishment? (If so, you teach your child to manipulate through shallow charm.)

Following through with consequences for bad behavior can be harder than providing appropriate clothing and nourishing meals, but it is just as essential. Like keeping your child warm, sheltered, and fed, follow-through demonstrates your commitment and love.

BEYOND CONSEQUENCES: ENGAGING YOUR TEEN'S *YETZER HARA*

Judaism is clear about the benefits of *teshuvah* for children who engage in the predictable process of testing society's limits. But Jewish teachings also describe a source of bad behavior that cannot be explained by simple ethical fieldwork. I'm talking about the concept I described in chapter 5: the *yetzer hara,* the evil inclination that exists in all of us. Although parents may wish they could snuff out their teen's *yetzer hara,* I don't advise it. The ancient rabbis believed that although the *yetzer hara* leads us to cause trouble, it is also the spark of life, responsible for every shining human achievement. Crush the *yetzer hara,* and you crush your child's spirit.

The *yetzer* takes different forms in different people. The form it takes in your child may be unfamiliar, strange, or frightening, but you must approach it with curiosity and without prejudice, because the *yetzer* contains *every* potential. Like fire, the *yetzer* can be used for good or evil. Like fire, it must be protected and respected, but not extinguished. Our job as parents is to help our children learn to use their *yetzer* for its best, noblest purposes—for creating, not destroying. As children get older, this process becomes progressively more terrifying. In a small child, the *yetzer*'s fire is just a flicker. There are tantrums, breath-holding, biting, fibbing, snatching, snitching, and squeezing the baby too hard—adorable problems, the kind a parent might be tempted to post on YouTube. But in a teenager, the *yetzer* is a four-alarm blaze. The *yetzer* has been known to wreck transcripts and reputations. It threatens to burn the bridges that lead to your child's future.

So how do you respect and protect your teen's raging *yetzer*? How can you protect his creativity and passion while helping him grow into a responsible adult? When your teen lies to you and then lies about the lie; when he shames the family or debases himself; when he cheats and steals, by all means impose consequences. But I also recommend that you look your teen's *yetzer hara* straight in the eye. Get to know it. Get on its good side, and put it to work. The process starts by identifying the unique nature of your child's *yetzer hara*.

Amelia and the Sexy Yetzer

Reports of fifteen-year-old Amelia's activities reached home via the daughter-to-mom-to-mom grapevine. Amelia had made out with two different boys at the cast party; further, she had not been studying in the library after school as she claimed but instead had been spending afternoons in the fraternity house dorm room of a boy named Nick.

Her father, Jeff, was furious about the lying. Her mother, Laurel, was ashamed by her daughter's public show of promiscuity. Laurel blamed herself: Why would Amelia sell herself so cheaply? What was lacking in their home? Of course, both parents were also worried about the consequences of Amelia's sexual behavior for her health and reputation.

As I discussed the problem with Laurel and Jeff, they agreed to some *teshuvah* for Laurel. Because Amelia had lied about her whereabouts, she would have to come clean with them about any other lies or half-truths she'd told them. More concretely, Amelia was grounded for a month. At the end of that time, Laurel and Jeff would reassess Amelia's trustworthiness. But I explained that I was also interested in another domain—in tracking down the qualities of Amelia's *yetzer hara*.

I often start this process by asking parents what caused their child to light up when she was small. Was she delighted by waves at the beach, or fireworks? Was music like a switch that started her twirling or singing? Did she like cutting and chopping? Did she like things sensual or sexy: a velvety blankie, running naked, getting a glimpse of the forbidden? Did she like to wander and explore? Was her room very tidy and organized, and did she do pretend "homework" in preschool? Act as the block captain of the neighborhood kids, creating groups and assigning each a set of duties and responsibilities? Or did she love to clown and make people laugh? Did she prefer to be cozy, wrapped up tight in a blanket with her three favorite stuffies? Was he a curious little person, persistent in his questions about "why people think that," and how things worked? The answers can help you reframe a child's current problem behavior as a vivid, new, teenaged illustration of their best qualities.

I asked Laurel and Jeff about what Amelia had loved to do when she was a buoyant first-grader, before hormones and academic and social pressures began to unsettle her. It took them a while to get rolling, but then the tales tumbled out. Amelia loved Play-Doh. Enchanted her younger cousins by making perfect tiny little ice cream cones, neatly swirled, plates of dinner with peas and corn, and a hot dog in a bun with a folded polka-dot Play-Doh napkin on the side. Amelia was also deeply devoted to her baby doll, Mary, who frequently came down with a cold and had to be rocked to sleep. Laurel and Jeff soon began to beam as they recalled their sensual, nurturing, imaginative daughter—the flip side of the provocative, sexually careless teen. We were well on our way to understanding Amelia's *yetzer hara.*

Identifying the unique nature of a teen's *yetzer hara* is a tricky exercise in vision, like trying to spot the surprising and beautiful three-dimensional images hidden in the Magic Eye posters and books. You have to relax your gaze in an unfamiliar manner. At first you see only the ordinary geometric patterns on the surface, but when you break the gestalt and look beyond the image, there you are in an entirely new scene. A dinosaur! Seven floating swans! Beautiful colored marbles!

So when, like Laurel and Jeff, your field of vision is narrowed by anger and discouragement, stop. Look around. This unfamiliar landscape has the potential to be dazzling; there is intelligence or courage or spirit driving your child's troubles. Try to see with greater dimension.

Just as Laurel and Jeff could look at Amelia's sexual behavior and see the affectionate, nurturing child inside, you can take another view of the big problems your child has caused.

A parent may complain, "My son drove the car over the speed limit and with a passel of friends when his junior license restricts him to driving without passengers for six more months. He got a speeding ticket, but was lucky he didn't have his license suspended. And he's stayed out past curfew three times this month." This activity can be a cue to recall the nature and temperament of the small child: *He was thrilled by the waves, fireworks.*

Here are some other possibilities:

- "We found out that Malcolm spent last Friday night with his girlfriend, watching Scooby-Doo cartoons, and eating marshmallows in his van parked just off Lake Shore Drive. When we asked him what he thought he was doing, he said, 'It was fun, like we were camping or homeless. Well, sort of.'" *He loved to be cozy and tucked in tight.*
- "She lies to us. She says she's at one friend's house but goes to parties with kids whose families we don't know." *Loved to wander and explore.*
- "He cheated on a test and got caught. Instead of studying, he spends hours making dopey YouTube videos with his dopey friends." *Loved clowning and being the center of attention.*
- "We found out she bullied other girls online." *Block captain of the kids, always creating groups.*
- "On the report card narrative his English teacher wrote, 'He can be challenging with his peers.' In our parent-teacher conference she told us he is so sure of his ideas that his behavior borders on rude." *So curious, endlessly asking "Why?" or "How does it work?"*

Once you've recalled the specifics of that good *yetzer* energy of childhood—your twirling, racing, clowning, questioning child—you can begin to engage that energy, helping your teen channel it in a more fruitful, satisfying direction.

Channeling the Yetzer Hara

Teens do best when they have constructive outlets for their unique and hard-charging *yetzers*. A girl with an outspoken, argumentative *yetzer* might question her school's limits on the student body's role in setting policies and galvanize fellow students to demand changes. A physically daring *yetzer* might like to spin, flip, and pop his long board at the skate park. What about Amelia? What were some outlets for her talents and natural inclinations, besides fooling around with boys who didn't mean much to her?

I mulled this over with Laurel and Jeff. How about baby-sitting? In that role she could be both queenly and of service. "Amelia's here! Look, Eli, she's wearing a braid! You never wore a braid before, right, Amelia? Can we make a Play-Doh dinner tonight for Mr. Mouse and Lucy?" Or what about theater, to satisfy her longing to be admired and special? Art class? Cooking school? We were on a roll. Then I reminded Laurel and Jeff that we were dealing with a tetchy teenager.

Avoid the Hard Sell

A teenager is protective and loyal to her *yetzer* because she views it as a precious aspect of her individuality. If Laurel said to Amelia, "Let's find some healthy outlets for all your wonderful talents," she'd most likely be met with "Uh, no thanks." Teens are naturally suspicious of parental suggestions of any type, especially those that appear to say: *You've got some bad qualities and we want to help you get rid of them ASAP.* To entice the *yetzer* down a new pathway, you need to be subtle and persistent. It also helps to play to your teen's narcissism, allowing her to see your ideas as her own.

Laurel suggested that Amelia audition for the spring musical. Amelia responded, "I don't like those theater kids. Any of them. They're too happy." Baby-sitting: "Gross. Kids puke and you have to change dirty diapers." But then Laurel abandoned her direct marketing. She casually mentioned that a new ceramics studio had opened at the craft center downtown:

I'm planning to drop by to see if they want to participate in the silent auction for the school fund-raiser, and on the way home I'll be passing by the mall, so if you want to look for new boots, I would be happy to take you to see what's in the stores.

Amelia responded flatly, "Yeah, I guess so."

Once at the studio, Laurel stretched out her conversation with the staff person for as long as possible while Amelia looked at the pottery.

Before they left, Amelia decided to sign up for a class. "I'm probably not going to like it," she warned Laurel.

Ceramics class, week one: *The other kids are bizarre. I'm not kidding. There's not one who is normal. I don't know where they find them. I keep waiting for them all to start singing "Ninety-Nine Luftballoons." And we're not going to be using the wheel for a month. We're just making little clay snakes. It's like lame-o kindergarten.*

Week two: *Well, I guess there's one girl who's okay.*

Week three: *There are these two girls I really like and we're making these really neat, really tall coiled candleholders. . . . I've made four of them in different heights. They look like a family. . . . Next week we're starting pinch pots. And the center is having an exhibit of Bauhaus pottery from England. We helped unpack the crates today after class.*

Week four: *The wheel sucks. It's too hard. There are two types of people in the world. Those who get it right away and those who never will.*

Week ten: *The studio is having a show of student work in December and my family of candleholders will be in it. Can you and Dad come? And can we invite Nonny and Poppa?*

It took nearly a semester, but eventually Amelia found sensuality, creativity, and a second home at the craft center—rather than in Nick's fraternity house.

Be Prepared to Cringe

Michael Resnick, activist professor of pediatrics and public health at the University of Minnesota, describes adolescents as "resources to be developed, not problems to be solved." Making friends with the *yetzer hara* means opening your mind and arms and heart to your child's talents and proclivities, even if they're not the ones you might wish him to possess. In order to help your child channel his *yetzer hara*, you may have to detach from the vision of life you've conjured up on your child's behalf. This approach enables you to welcome whatever muddy treasures the *yetzer* might drag in. Be prepared for a well-channeled *yetzer* to emerge as a passion for something that makes you cringe: death metal, cheerleading, veganism, touch football, ROTC, crowd surfing, extreme Zionism, or even having a tiny part in the school musical season after season. Just smile, be curious about whatever it is your teen is doing, and fight the urge to ask, "How will you describe this activity on your college application?"

Remember, too, that the face of the *yetzer* today (ceramics at the craft center) may not be the face you'll see next month or next year:

Hey, Mom, I'm doing layout for the student newspaper. No, not that one, the underground paper. It's called RATS, and our motto is "Responsibility without AuthoriTy is Slavery." Matt's dad knows a lawyer who works for the ACLU who is going to help us fight the administration's ban on distributing it. Obviously, the ban is a violation of our First Amendment rights. Anyone can see that.

Right at that moment, say "Oy" to yourself. Say "Oy" frequently. Then remind yourself: There is no aboveground or underground paper without talent, inspiration, hard work, and commitment. That the *yetzer hara* is varied, colorful, different, and *tov meod* (very good).

WHEN YOU CAN'T DO IT YOURSELF

There are times when a teen's unethical behavior cannot be explained by ethical fieldwork or the normal exuberance of the *yetzer hara,* times when his pattern of choices signals the need for outside help.

Healthy teens blame other people for their mistakes, sprinkle their truths with lies, prefer deviousness to direct defiance, lose their tempers, and do all they can to avoid responsibilities they find onerous . . . but not all the time. Pay attention if your child's sentences frequently begin with "I have no idea why" and end with the claim that he has been wrongfully blamed for something he says he didn't do, or didn't mean, or isn't responsible for. Also take note if explanations such as "bad coincidences," "just the wrong place at the wrong time, I guess," or "discrimination" appear to be a reflex response to any sort of trouble.

I have no idea how my bike (or laptop, or cell phone) got stolen again!

I have no idea why this jerk at the party and his two friends started the fight, but I had to defend myself.

I have no idea why I've been banned from the skate park.

I have no idea why Mr. King says I didn't hand in four assignments, because I did. Everyone knows he loses things, just ask them.

That girl was chasing me the whole night. I didn't force her to do anything she didn't want to.

I didn't mean to hurt him [little brother, the dog]. We were just playing.

Teens who *chronically, consistently* fail to accept responsibility for their actions are not typical.

Parents can become so accustomed to their child's extreme behavior that they no longer see it. The most reliable signs that your teen's problems fall outside the ordinary range of adolescent experimentation may come from outside sources, especially educators. Professionals who work with teenagers have a long and broad view, so if your child's teacher suggests that he is having significant trouble, take it seriously. Also watch for telltale signs from other kids. When siblings fear being alone with their older brother or sister, or when old friends drop him, evaluate the situation carefully. Be aware of your own reactions, too, and recognize that it's not normal for you to be afraid of your own child, to feel that you have to lock up money or substances when your child is home, or to avoid taking family vacations because your teen makes the rest of you miserable. In these circumstances, your child's behavior may be an SOS. Therapy can help you decode that distress call.

THE EXAMPLE YOU SET

I conclude almost every lecture with the same quote. It's from a seventeenth-century Chassidic rabbi, Menachem Mendel of Kotzk: "If you truly wish your child to study Torah, study it yourself in his presence. He will follow your example. Otherwise he will not himself study Torah, but will simply instruct his children to do so." Why am I still dragging this quote around a few hundred lectures after finding it? Why not find something jazzy and new?

Because setting an example for children instead of telling them what to do is so very difficult. And of all the examples we wish to set, behaving with integrity is the most important.

In my travels to schools around the country, I hear jaw-dropping stories about parents who commit unethical acts in the name of helping their children:

A college placement counselor called a family to discuss whether their daughter would be better served by an Early Decision rather than an Early Action application to her first-choice school. The counselor's call was returned seconds later.

"The parents call me back so quickly. I feel like I have a red phone at the White House," she told me. In this case, the caller was the student's father. Some strange noises in the background made it a bit difficult to hear him.

"What's that noise?" my counselor friend asked.

"Oh, nothing," the father quickly reassured her. "It's fine. I can talk. I'm just doing a colonoscopy."

The counselor, sputtering, told him she would prefer to continue the conversation later.

Another father, pretending to be his son, forged an e-mail to the boy's teacher contesting his grade on an English midterm. (His ploy failed. The teacher knew his student's writing style and recognized an imposter.)

A different college counselor told me about a call she made to congratulate a senior on her revised application essay.

"I see you decided to add your experience with your cousin to your essay. I was really moved by what you wrote," said the counselor.

"What?"

"The trip you took to the Grand Canyon with your autistic cousin."

"Oh my God." The girl's voice lost its lilt. Suddenly she sounded like a world-weary adult. "I know what happened. I'll take care of it." Her mother had rewritten the essay to include this story and inserted it into the application without telling her daughter.

"The scary thing was that she immediately knew what her mom had done," the adviser told me. "Her tone said, 'Here we go again.'"

When I use these examples in lectures, audience members gasp in shared horror over the behavior of Those Awful Parents. I then say to them, "It's easy to see the folly in these extreme acts, but what about the rest of us? Which rules do we break? What excuses do we make? And what is the impact on our children?"

Teenagers appear to pay little attention to their parents. They are preoccupied and distant; their heads are always down, reading the cell phone display. But don't be fooled. Teens study all your moves. They will be quick to pick up on your hypocrisy and use it to justify their own elastic definitions of right and wrong.

Take advantage of the freedom you have now that your teen doesn't want to spend as much time with you as she did when she was little. Use it to work on yourself. Study the gaps between what you say and what you do.

- Do you violate the school's carpool drop-off and pickup rules, yet expect your children to follow rules at home?
- Do you encourage a twelve-year-old to say she is eleven to qualify for a lower-priced movie ticket, yet feel incensed if you discover she has shoplifted?
- Do you shout at your children but become indignant if your teenager raises her voice at an adult?
- Do you gossip about friends, family, neighbors, or school personnel, yet expect your children to be kind to their siblings?
- Do you demand frugality from your teen but spend beyond your means on vacations, your wardrobe, or electronics?
- Do you say you're sick and can't go to work or attend a social event when a more appealing opportunity presents itself, and then expect your teen to show up at school every day of the second semester of their senior year?

Teenagers are reluctant but clever students of behavioral ethics. As a parent you will need to tailor your lesson plan to each child and the specific nature of her *yetzer hara*. You'll need to use trial and error to determine the most effective way for her to express her inclinations and make up for wrongdoing. The reward for devoting yourself to this curriculum, for writing and rewriting, for getting consultation and expert help as needed, does not arrive as immediate gratification. It's best expressed by the story of Honi the Circle Maker, as told by Peninnah Schram, a *maggid* (master storyteller and collector of Jewish tales) in her 2008 book, *The Hungry Clothes and Other Jewish Folktales:*

One day, as Honi the Circle Maker was walking down the road, he saw an old man planting a carob tree. After greeting the man, Honi asked him, "How long will it take for this tree to bear fruit?"

The old man replied, "Seventy years."

Then Honi asked the old man, "And do you think you will live long enough to eat the fruit of this tree?"

The old man answered, "Perhaps not. But when I was born, I found many carob trees planted by my father and grandfather. Just as they planted trees for me, I am planting trees for my children and grandchildren so that they will be able to enjoy eating the trees' fruit. Then it will be up to them to plant more trees for future generations."

When we undertake the difficult job of planting good values in our teenagers, we are investing in the lives of our grandchildren. The ethics we pass along to our children are the ones they will pass on to their children. We want our children to be honest, compassionate, patient, brave, and considerate toward others. And if given the opportunity to perform a colonoscopy, we want them to put the school counselor on hold.

CHAPTER 9

The Blessing of a Hangover:

A Sanctified Approach to Substances and Sex

Somewhere in America last June, two twelfth-grade boys hosted a post-prom "after party" in a rented nightclub. The boys charged forty dollars for admission and hired a DJ, strippers, and security guards; most students had fake IDs that easily fooled the bartender. When the girls got too drunk to stand, bouncers dragged them to a makeshift infirmary. The rumor was that many students got stoned, and some had sex in the limousines on the way home. The hosts netted about fifteen thousand dollars, and the students who attended the party reported that they had a wonderful time.

Somewhere else in America, a few high school students made a pornographic video starring themselves. It was an accident, they claimed— two kids just fooling around, and someone had a camera. Accident or not, the video was screened in the boys' locker room.

Right here in my neighborhood, a tenth grader hosted a party at her home. There was a guest list of forty. Her parents planned to keep a close eye on the activities, but when news of the party spread via text messages and phone calls, other kids started flowing in from around town. By ten o'clock, close to one hundred teenagers had surged past the astonished adults into the house. By eleven o'clock, two fifteen-year-olds lay passed out on the floor outside an upstairs bathroom. One had to have her stomach pumped. The doctor said she was near death from alcohol poisoning.

Sex, drugs, alcohol. Incidents such as these leave adults quaking. What can be done, they wonder, to prevent such Caligula-style excess?

When word got out about the nightclub after-party, school officials met with parents to discuss what had gone wrong. The discussion instantly turned prickly, as parents and administrators argued about what should be done to prevent future bacchanals. Some demanded a public rebuke of the boys who hosted the party; others wanted to cast blame on the parents who allowed their teens to attend. Some parents argued that the school should discontinue proms, thereby assuring that there would be no after-parties, limousines, or fake IDs. Another parental contingent took the approach that if drugs and teenaged drinking were legalized, kids wouldn't have to take their consumption underground. The school psychologist blamed the media. When Madonna and Britney Spears kiss at the MTV Music Awards in a crass bid to increase ratings, she said, how can we expect our students to behave with decorum and modesty? She suggested that parents should direct their teens' attention toward more wholesome entertainment.

To a certain extent, all the forces named by the parents are culpable: irresponsible teens, weak-willed parents, unrealistic laws, Madonna and Britney. But extreme solutions, such as shutting down the prom or wholesale drug legalization, are the easy and dangerous ways out. More difficult is inserting yourself into the tangle of these embarrassing, frightening, and delicate subjects with your teen, and figuring out how to make rules and have conversations about sex, drugs, and alcohol that are consistent with her changing level of maturity. This task is so daunting because many parents aren't sure where *they* stand on these topics. They aren't sure that abstention works, but they don't want to endorse raunchy excess, either. The Jewish principle of moderation provides welcome clarity.

GOD WANTS US TO PLANT GRAPEVINES

Certainly the ancient Jewish philosophers recognized the dangers of overindulgence. They made laws against gluttony and inebriation, and pointed out that vivid, cautionary tales about people who lack self-control appear in the very first book of the Bible. One minute God creates the world and puts all sorts of lovely, fresh, wholesome stuff in it that is "pleasing to the sight," and the next minute he puts a restriction on its enjoyment. He offers every single pleasure to Adam and Eve *except for one thing:* the apples from that tree over there.

Of course, this limitation makes that tree, and those homely apples, particularly alluring. Although Adam and Eve are encouraged to experience sensory delight in every other corner of Eden, they cannot discipline themselves to refuse the apple. From there, things go downhill, and (in the quick version) humanity eventually slides into hedonism. God decides to throw out his first draft of civilization—to flood it—and start over. He asks the world's only righteous man, Noah, to build an ark. There's a lot of rain, the raven flies, the dove flies, and a beautiful rainbow appears. God offers Noah and his family a fresh start on new dry land. But had God planned for a new world with no wine and no juice, just crackers and water?

No, according to the biblical commentary, God commanded Noah to bring saplings and branches for grapevines *onto the ark,* right along with the animals. The first thing Noah, tiller of the soil, did after the flood was plant a vineyard. Next thing we know he's drunk, passed out, and lying half-naked in his tent. When his sons come upon him, two of them cover him in his shame. Despite this excess, God never suggests that Noah should pull up his vineyard or even stop drinking. Planting grapes, making wine, and celebrating with alcohol is seen as a sign of civilization in this new, post-deluvian world.

Alcohol occupies an honored position in the Jewish faith. God asks us to use wine as a sacrament at the altar and as an essential element of every ritual, whether in the synagogue or at home. The "kiddush" (meaning "sanctification"), which is recited to usher in Shabbat and other festivals, is a blessing made over wine to symbolize the transformation of secular time—the weekday—into holy time. There are also specific laws requiring *hiddur mitzvah* (beautification of a mitzvah), in which we are commanded to elevate Shabbat and holidays through special food, flowers on the table, and more wine. In Ecclesiastes we read: *Go, eat your bread in gladness and drink your wine in joy, for your action was long ago approved by God.*

WHY ABSTINENCE IS RUDE TO GOD

The proper use of wine was encouraged in Jewish tradition; it is abstinence that was seen as dangerous. Look at the unusual rules governing the behavior of the Nazarite. The Nazarite (from *nazir,* a Hebrew word meaning "set aside" or "dedicated") is a person who takes an ascetic vow not to drink wine, cut his or her hair, or attend funerals. (Interestingly, even Nazarites are not permitted to refrain from sex.) But this period of abstinence is usually short, about a month, and when it's over, the Nazarite marks his transition back to the world with a lavish offering to God, including the traditional sin offering of a ewe. Why such a big production, why a sin offering after a period of abstinence?

Because in the Babylonian Talmud, we read that abstinence is potentially as dangerous as forbidden indulgences:

One who imposes vows of abstinence upon himself is as though he puts an iron collar around his neck; he is like one who builds a prohibited altar; he is like one who takes a sword and plunges it into his heart. Sufficient for you is what the Torah forbids. Do not seek to add further restrictions.

The iron collar is a metaphor for a shortcut method of protecting against overindulgence. If you have a big heavy ring around your neck, you don't have to decide whether to have a glass of wine; you can barely bend your head back to inhale the wonderful aroma. If you abstain for too long, you could find yourself building a "prohibited altar," meaning that you worship your own self-control. (Women and girls who suffer from anorexia are prone to a similar moral superiority. While there are many complex motivations for this heartbreaking condition, one is a form of elevation: *I have transcended my body, unlike you gluttonous mortals.*) The "sword" is the pain of denying yourself the opportunity to appreciate the products of nature. And there's more. The rabbis go on to caution that abstinence might separate you from your community and from the celebrations and rituals that knit people together. Abstinence is a spiritual shortcut that prevents us from living fully, just as crash dieting is a shortcut around sensible eating.

(The rabbis understood that drinking is off limits to some of us, so they made an exception if "wine is not tolerated or medically inadvisable." In this case, abstinence is permitted, but one is then required to substitute other sensory pleasures, such as especially flavorful foods, for alcohol.)

An attitude of moderation means that parents cannot attempt to shut down their child's capacity for pleasure by barking "Just say no!" whenever he is tempted. Nor can we turn a blind eye toward debauchery and dangerous activities. But is it possible to teach moderation to teenagers, people who are in a naturally immoderate stage of life? When parents ask me, "Isn't it prudent to frighten my risk-loving, hormonally challenged teen into not engaging in any of these dangerous activities, ever? Isn't it better to keep teenagers on a short leash and away from any possibility of noxious influences?" I respond, "If you do not teach them moderation now, when will they learn it? And from whom?"

VICE TEACHES LIFE SKILLS

One argument against a strict, abstinence-is-the-only-policy approach to teaching kids about sex and substances is that it usually doesn't work. Have you ever sat in on a middle school class on drug and alcohol awareness? A police officer or the district attorney gazes out at the eighth graders and says: "One in four of you will die from drugs or alcohol before your twenty-first birthday." Or, to the girls: "You think boys aren't slipping roofies into the beer they offer you? Think again. One sip and you'll end up a date-rape statistic." Things aren't any better when teens take sex education in health class. The information is absurdly cold and clinical, with an emphasis on scare tactics and statistics: "Just one careless, drunken act at a party and you'll die from AIDS!"

Possible? Yes. Likely? No. And the kids know this. Like those of us who watched the old anti-marijuana film *Reefer Madness* in school, they write the whole message off, throwing out the helpful information along with the nonsense. They can't wait to leave the classroom and start making jokes about the dumb lecture.

As parents, it's tempting to take a zero-tolerance approach toward sex and substances. But that is the same miscalculation the just-say-no lecturers make. Whether parents like it or not, it's normal for most kids to do some drinking at parties during the last two years of high school. Depending on the region of the country and local mores, it's also typical for kids to try some pot. Although slightly more than half of teens graduate from high school without having had sexual intercourse, there are, obviously, many who do. And because puberty occurs earlier than it did in our generation, some kids have sex earlier.

It's better to be realistic than naive about what you can and cannot control. If you are too shocked or moralizing, you will not prevent teen experimentation; you will simply drive it underground. Teens who are afraid of being punished or humiliated will cut you out of the conversation—a serious problem, because they badly need your advice. If they don't get it from you, they will turn to their peers: the morally blind leading the morally blind.

An even more compelling reason to avoid a prim and punitive stance with your kids is that it's good for them to have some experience with substances and sexual behavior before they head off to college. At this point, the parents I counsel usually say something like, "What about the danger? The diseases? The trouble with the law? Excuse me, but what benefit could there possibly be to experimentation?"

The benefit is the opportunity for teens to develop self-knowledge and risk management skills while they are still under their parents' care. To learn how their minds, bodies, and spirits react to a rum and Coke, or two rum and Cokes. To understand how awful it feels to walk down the school hallway on the Monday after Will told all his soccer teammates that you made out with him on Friday night. To realize: *Oh, I'm a lot like Uncle Rob. When I drink I don't feel like I'm drunk. Now I see how he ended up with a DUI.*

I want all of this to happen while teens are living at home, getting a decent amount of sleep on most nights, and eating regular meals. I want them to experience making mistakes under the watchful eye of a parent, one who is willing to provide comfort and guidance and consequences when appropriate.

Sounds like you'll want to move slower next time. To protect against regret.

Who can brainstorm ways to prevent the mistake from happening again:

Can you come up with a plan to get through finals without high doses of Red Bull or extra ADHD medication? Remember what happened last time.

Who can make rules according to a child's demonstrated level of maturity:

Because of some of your recent decisions, we have decided to take away your car keys.

Who can recognize when a child is sinking and stage a rescue:

Your grades have been dropping and I noticed that your eyes have been glassy the last couple of times you've come home at night. Something's not right here. I called a counselor who works with teens and made an appointment for a family meeting tomorrow at five-thirty.

If your child waits until college to mess around with powerful stuff, who will say these things to him? Possibly no one. At college your child will talk to adults about Shakespeare and macroeconomic theory and Chinese martial arts in cinema, but not about how to drink prudently or how sex can damage a fragile new relationship or elevate a loving one. Mostly, they'll talk about sex and substances to other students, who will say things like:

How do you know you won't like it until you've tried it?

Let's play beer pong.

I've never met anybody who can party like you. You're already a school legend.

For some kids, middle and high school experimentation with drinking, drugs, and sex will be minimal. They won't do more than put a tentative toe in the water. For others it will be a big, hearty swim in a deep sea. But once teens are in college, the siren call of indulgence is so powerful that the child who has been frightened or shamed out of *any* trial and error can be sucked under. So can the child who has behaved recklessly and never experienced any consequences. This is why the school years are the ideal opportunity for your child to learn the difference between a misstep (drinking much too fast when you're lonely at a party and then making out with a boy you don't really like) and fun moderation (getting tipsy at the cast party or sharing an intimate moment in the backseat with a boyfriend who is sweet and devoted).

It's scary, I know. Parents who try to calibrate the scales of delight and safety have to account for normal teenage curiosity, hormones, love of breaking rules, omnipotence, and the exhilaration of taking risks. How can parents negotiate a smooth transition from the safety and supervision of home to the garden full of apple trees, snakes, and vineyards?

GOOD "TRUTHINESS"

I absolutely do not suggest that parents, in an attempt to avoid shutting down the conversation about physical pleasures, swing to the other extreme: cool parenthood.

Cool parents serve alcohol at teen parties, host coed slumber parties, or even invite their kids to smoke pot with them. While these activities can be rationalized, none of them is appropriate or safe. Cool parents say, "Wait a minute! My parents disapproved of everything, but that never stopped me. I did all kinds of dangerous and illegal stuff when I was his age and I made it through okay. So why lay down silly, empty restrictions we know he isn't going to follow?"

These are fair questions. Here are my answers: because your job as a parent is to show respect for the laws and conventions of the society in which you are raising your child. Because even brilliant teenagers are too inexperienced and reckless to make fine distinctions between *this* illegal or dangerous activity and *that* one. If you break laws with them at home, they will see it as an invitation to do so elsewhere. And in order to protect their identities as rebellious, no-one-can-tell-me-what-to-do adolescents, they may have to push the envelope beyond whatever it is that their parents tolerate. Because teens need to understand that sloppy or excessive sex or substance use leads to outcomes for which they will find themselves paying a disagreeable or irreversible price.

If being too strict or too cool doesn't work, what does? The formula I offer parents is one of mild "truthiness." This means you recognize that teen experimentation is normal, even desirable, but you don't share this information with your teen. Why not? Because in their confusing world, teens need to hear a clear parental voice. Give them rules about safety and decency, making these boundaries fairly conservative with young teens and allowing more freedom as teens mature. Talk to your teen frequently about these charged subjects. Again, adopt some truthiness. Do not endorse risky behavior, but recognize and accept that it's probably going to happen. Let that unspoken awareness inform your conversations. Give them the information they need to stay safe. Let them know that you are always willing to listen without rushing to judgment, to help them weigh their options when they are in trouble, and to offer the voice of experience.

MAKING FAIR, APPROPRIATE RULES ABOUT SEX AND SUBSTANCES

With young teens (from middle school to tenth grade), making rules about sex and substances is a straightforward procedure. Young teens are still so cognitively, emotionally, and physically immature that it's better for them to wait as long as possible to do much more than take a tentative swig of beer or play the current version of Spin the Bottle or Truth or Dare. Don't make unrealistic blanket "never ever" statements—you can never ever take a drink until you are twenty-one, never ever be alone with a person of the opposite sex—but let them know that drugs, drinking, and sex are not safe or sensible at this age. Make rules that let you stand dull and tall and consistent:

You are not permitted to drink at parties.

You are not permitted to attend parties where no adult is present.

We don't want you home with your boyfriend when no adult is in the house, and your door must remain open when he is in your room.

I heard about what happened with Brett and Eli on the camping trip. If we found out that you were smoking pot we would be very surprised and disappointed. And there would be serious consequences.

Then you say in a gentle, respectful tone of voice: "Do you understand what I said? Please repeat it back to me so I'm sure you get it."

As teens reach their junior and senior years, these tactics become too simple. At this age, teens are statistically much more likely to experiment, and they are often mature enough to take some precautions. Your stance becomes even more "truthy" *(I am setting rules even though I know the chances are good that you will break them),* but it doesn't benefit anyone if you clamp down too hard. You allow more freedom to participate in unsupervised situations, but you dole out this freedom gingerly, with a keen eye on your unique child and his ever-changing needs. I recommend that you once again examine your teen in the natural laboratories of his life. Take a good look at your teen *as he is right now.* Is he a bit careless and slippery, or is he mostly responsible and forthright? Then consider the situation your child wishes to put him or herself in. Now do the math. If your child seems equal to the circumstances, give your assent, and make it specific:

I know you and Caleb and Martin want to work on the history project after school. It's fine with me if you follow all the house rules.

I know from your sister's experience that the Goldmans don't keep a close eye on the kids' parties. I also remember when we were all there for Theo's big birthday. We sat around drinking wine and eating, and it was fun, but things got too wild as the evening wore on. I'm going to let you go, but I'm not so comfortable with it. I'm trusting you to leave if the party gets out of control. You don't have to give any reason; just walk out the door.

You boys can go on the road trip. It sounds like fun, but I want you to text me when you get there and when you set out for home.

If the challenge of your child's proposed plan (casually supervised party at home where alcohol will almost certainly be served, teen driver, hours of "home alone" time after school for young teen sweethearts) doesn't meet your teenager's current resources (natural temperament, level of maturity, mood during the last couple of weeks), don't agree to it. You don't always have to explain your reasoning, either. Use the dependable phrase "I'm not ready" to sidestep a protracted debate.

There's a good chance that everything would turn out fine, but I'm not ready for . . .

> *you to go to a party at Colin's house.*
> *Derrick to drive four kids home.*
> *you and Ella to work on your project at home instead of at the library at school.*

They may storm off and be mad at you, but often they are relieved to know an adult is in charge. When they are with their friends, they can pass around your superego like a business card: "I would go to Jonah's, but my mom wants me to be a social outcast." Even when your teen does not appreciate your rules one bit, coolly enforcing them is your hard job, day in and day out. And it sends a message about your love of this child and your respect for his need for fun *and* his need for protection. Repeat this to yourself daily.

RULES ARE NOT ENOUGH

No matter how well you adjust the rules for your teen's unique needs, you do not have control—not complete control anyway—over whether and how much your teen drinks or smokes or makes out or has sex. This is why you need to open the door to conversation. Not confession, not spin, but conversation.

If your teen comes to you for advice, be honored. Demonstrate your respect by listening to the whole story. Don't immediately cluck or go into embarrassed or stern and shocked mode. If you do, they'll react by closing down or opposing you. And be aware that sometimes teens hand us their problems so that they can avoid dealing with them. If you respond too emotionally, they're almost relieved. Instead of figuring out how to solve the problem, they can simply react to your reaction:

Teen: *I have something to tell you, Mom. I need birth control.*
Mom: *You may never see Alec again.*
Teen: *Oh my God! Why did I trust you? I'm never telling you anything again!*

Teen: *I have something to tell you, Mom. Courtney's doing coke.*
Mom: *I'm calling her mother right away!*
Teen: *No! You can't! Oh my God. I'm never telling you anything again.*

Slow down. Do not react in fear. Listen without lecturing, and without interrupting. Ask some open-ended questions. One of your jobs is to help her deepen her understanding of the situation and the role she wishes to take in it.

Teen: *Alec asked me to spend the night with him.*
Mom: *Whoa. I guess I'm a little surprised. Let's sit down. What do you think about this?*

Teen: *Courtney's doing coke.*
Mom: *Wow. I'm sad to hear that. What do you think is going on? (Or, How is it affecting your friendship? How is it affecting her?)*

Then hand the problem back to your teen. Say, "What are you planning to do?"

You may need to ask questions that suggest your mutual ability to come up with a good solution. Does she want some ideas for talking to Courtney? Does she need something intelligent and honest to say to Alec? Does she need to see a doctor about birth control? Help her evaluate her options—and only *then* should you weigh in with your point of view. Depending on the situation and your teen's maturity, you may eventually decide that adult action is called for. You may choose to call Courtney's mother, or to make rules about unsupervised dates with Alec. Weigh these decisions carefully, knowing that if you sidestep your bond with your teen too swiftly or indelicately, she may hesitate to tell you anything too fraught again. But if your teen finds you a good listener when she's faced with a minor pickle, she'll feel more confident coming to you if she faces more serious troubles.

Not only must you be prepared to listen well, you must be prepared to initiate some conversations with your teen—about self-protection, about moderation, about ethics, about respect for others. I know actually having conversations with your child about drinking, drugs, and sex is more difficult than prescribing that you have one. The black-and-white, just-say-no approach is so pervasive that parents lack practice articulating the subtleties of responsible use. For conversations about drugs and drinking, I've found the concept of "set and setting" to be a useful opener. On the topic of sex, a good starter is to address the cheap values teens are exposed to in the media.

SET AND SETTING

The idea of "set and setting" is not something your teen will be taught in health education class. Partly because it suggests that there are times when teens can safely enjoy substances, and partly because I've borrowed it from Timothy Leary's 1964 book, *The Psychedelic Experience: A Manual Based on the Tibetan Book of the Dead.* I'm not advocating psychedelics for teens, but if you extract the basic principle and leave the LSD behind, what's left is a remarkably sturdy test for the appropriate use of alcohol or other substances. You can describe this concept to your teen, tailoring it to her age, her crowd, and her level of self-control and self-awareness.

In set and setting, the "set" describes your mind-set—your mood and state of mind—and "setting" describes your physical and social environment. In general, you want to drink only to enhance your mind-set, not to change it, and you want to drink when the setting is safe and friendly. Although adults may not think consciously about these calculations, they use the "set and setting" test all the time: *Did I have a big dinner, or is my stomach empty? How will I get home? What are my obligations tomorrow? Do I want to be careful to stay in control because this is a school fund-raiser, or can I really, really relax because we are on a kids-free vacation on a tropical island and rum drinks go so well with the sunset?*

Now let's think about teens and how they can apply set and setting to their lives. Mostly they will be tempted to do the opposite, to drink to change their mood, especially because they're often in social circumstances that feel new or uncomfortable. Their identity is still fluid and fragile. They go to a party and wonder: *Am I still in the group? How did my hair get that weird bump on one side? Why did I buy this shiny dress? Was what I just said totally ridiculous?* The liquid courage of alcohol helps steady their nerves, but it also prevents them from developing social skills, from learning that:

If that crowd ignores me I can join another one.
Everyone is nervous at the beginning of a party, but then you start to relax.
Whenever I start dancing I start to feel happier.

Some kids violate set and setting regularly. Some drink hard on the weekends to escape their weekday pressure—like sailors on liberty, they have only a few nights to blow off steam before returning to active duty, the duty of building their transcripts for college admissions. Others drink out of boredom: With so many exciting trips and activities, so much enrichment in general, the bar of excitement is raised and they find it hard to feel any invigoration without drugs or alcohol. Some teens use drunkenness as a free pass for lack of inhibition. ("I'm not responsible for what I said or did. I was wasted.") Some take drugs to make friends or impress.

Consider talking about your own experiences with set and setting. Be factual, not alarmist. You can say something like, *The worst times I had drinking were when I overdid it because I was . . .*

> *at the lake house of a really rich girl and I didn't feel like I fit in.*
> *in love with a boy who was at the party with another girl.*
> *upset about my midterm grades and afraid of my parents' reaction.*
> *trying to keep up with friends. I remember a drinking game where everyone did a shot whenever Suzanne Pleshette said "Hi, Bob" on reruns of* The Bob Newhart Show. *I got so sick it really scared me.*

Just be careful about telling your tales with too much relish and swagger. They might reinforce your teenager's natural sense of invulnerability.

You may not like the way your child responds. They may listen to your near-misses with a snide, "But you're okay now, aren't you?" Or to stories of a schoolmate who died or was injured with a dismissive, "So that's why you're so paranoid!" But they are listening. Don't expect them to say, "Wow, that's scary!" Or "I hear you." They may not even realize that what you are saying is making an impression, but assume it is. Even when it seems to be lost between their ears, your message is being stored away. Depending on the age and maturity of your teen, you can also use the "set and setting" test to describe occasions—after a big win, at a graduation party, at your older cousin's house, times when there was no need to drive home—where you did a modest or hearty amount of imbibing and came to no harm.

A natural opportunity to discuss a sanctified application of the principle of set and setting is during Jewish rituals, when wine is used to elevate and lubricate the fellowship of close family and friends. This includes splashy events such as weddings as well as the weekly Shabbat dinner. In this context, parents can teach teens the habits of healthy drinking just as they teach them about eating their meal before dessert or brushing their teeth before bed. Older children and teens, who are traditionally given a tiny amount of wine in their kiddush cups, learn the importance of drinking on a full stomach, of drinking in small sips, and of drinking moderate amounts lest—see your Uncle Ed?—you make a fool of yourself. Most of all, the teenager learns that drinking is ennobled by the purpose, the context, and the company. The toast *l'chaim*, familiar to Jews and non-Jews alike, is lyrical, jubilant. It means *Wow, life!* And the words carry with them whatever special meaning you wish to add, including: *Isn't it great to be here? Together! Celebrating the Sabbath! Aren't we happy right now? Being Jews! Being a family!* This is set and setting at its highest. This is the opposite of getting smashed at a party to mask your loneliness. It's the opposite of doing twenty-one Jell-O shots on your twenty-first birthday and ending up in the emergency room.

Sex: Talk Often but Not Much

Talking about sex offers some different challenges. No matter what your teen's current sexual status, and even if your teen's sexual life is confined to fantasy, the following is true: If you don't teach them your values, they will pick up their information from—as our parents used to say—"the street." Except that "the street" is now the wide boulevard of the information superhighway. As Dr. Ruth Westheimer notes in her up-to-date book *Dr. Ruth's Guide to Teens and Sex Today: From Social Networking to Friends with Benefits,* the extreme sexual practices found on pornography websites can exert a form of peer pressure on teens, especially if they haven't learned from more reliable sources about what constitutes typical, normal sex. Or they will learn about sex from the opportunistic sexuality of celebrities—back to Madonna and Britney—seeking media attention.

Teens may also pick up on the cultural approval of hookups (casual sexual contacts). Hookups and "friends with benefits" can be wildly appealing to teenagers, even to girls. Today's girls have sky-high ambitions, they rarely get enough sleep, they have girlfriends to provide emotional sustenance . . . why not just outsource sexual hunger to a friendly acquaintance? Although few parents would admit as much, I suspect that some of them quietly condone these quick, uncomplicated packets of release. This attitude puts desire into a neat compartment, like the little sleeping shelves in Japanese airports. Hop in, catch some zzz's, get on with your travels. But the sleep on those airport shelves is not as restful as what you'd get in a proper bed, and a hookup is never as deep or as nourishing as a relationship with someone you get to know well.

When parents fail to talk seriously to their teens about sex and love, teens may default to casual or extreme sex instead of cultivating a relationship that allows them to acquire mature sexual values or the skills of commitment: the ups and downs, the building of trust, the correction of misunderstandings, the practice of putting another person first. In *How Do I Decide? A Contemporary Jewish Approach to What's Right and Wrong,* Rabbi Roland B. Gittlesohn's book for teenagers about making ethical decisions, he describes sexual values with great depth when he says, "If you express yourself sexually only for physical stimulation you will experience release but not fulfillment. But if sexual expression is enriched by love and understanding you can have the deep satisfaction of joining the spiritual and emotional with the physical." We shape our behavior to elevate God's name, not to desecrate it. When sex is expressed in the proper context, it gives us the opportunity to express the divine image within us.

Certainly, most teenagers would choose a week of forced labor over

Mom or Dad's "Sex Is Wonderful Within a Loving, Committed Relationship" speech. Try talking about it and watch their eyes widen as they search for the nearest exit. So how do you approach the topic and deliver the necessary information?

Remember when your child was young, how you learned to answer only the question being asked:

Where did I come from?
Well, the sperm comes from . . .
No, was I born at Cedars-Sinai like Jaden or did I . . . ?

Or a bit later in childhood, when they learn how the sperm gets to the egg:

Oh, that's sooo gross! You mean you and Daddy did that two times?
At least.

Teens also need to receive education about sex in small doses. The information is complex and they are easily embarrassed and overwhelmed. But you can find lots of opportunities to bring up the general topic of sex and commitment and respect and have a brief back-and-forth discussion. You can do this when you talk about the news of public or fictional teen pregnancies: Jamie Lynn Spears, Bristol Palin, Juno from the eponymous movie, or Amy on *The Secret Life of the American Teenager*. Ask your child how she thinks the lives of young women change when they have a baby; talk about how some girls imagine that a baby will be like a tiny beautiful doll who will love and look up to them but that the reality is that the girls don't finish school or the grandmother ends up caring for the child. Talk about the media's hunger to expose sex scandals, or talk about abortion laws on the ballot when you vote. Make your home a pretty freewheeling chat room.

Using care not to sound preachy, deconstruct the sex ethics of television, movies, and the Internet. If you are watching television with your teen and see characters having sex an hour or two after meeting for the first time, you can use the opportunity to talk about hookups and commitment. You can say, kind of aloud to yourself: "They always hop right into bed on these shows. It makes the story more dramatic but it also makes people think that this is what people do in real life. They don't, just like they don't really escape the police after leading them on car chases." With older teens, ask their opinion. In this case, you are not trawling for spontaneous self-disclosure from your teenager, so no trick questions, please. Develop your curiosity about the point of view of an astute young person close to the issues:

Parent: *Is the "hookup culture" they show on TV an accurate reflection of what life is like for your friends?*

Daughter: *I guess.*

Parent: *What's your opinion of that? Do you see advantages in it? Disadvantages? When I was growing up there was a double standard for boys and girls. Is that still true?*

Daughter: *Yes, totally. If a guy and a girl hook up with the same number of people, the girl is called a skank and the guy is just a guy.*

Parent: *What leads a girl to do that, then? Do you think they are looking for love or attention or trying to rebel?*

Daughter: *Why aren't you asking that about the guy? Should she have to change her behavior just because the culture is giving her that label?*

Parent: *I was just thinking about the price she pays, but I see your point.*

Now close the case unless your daughter responds. If you know when to stay mum, you'll retain the privilege of revisiting the subject later.

Return to the technique of asking questions when subjects naturally present themselves. For example, when the subject of school dress codes comes up:

Son: *I can't believe it! Shauna got sent home today for violating the ridiculous dress code.*

Mom: *What was the violation?*

Son: *Bra straps, Mom; it's insane. I didn't know we lived in a totalitarian state. I thought we had constitutional rights. It's the new assistant principal. He's such an asshole.*

Mom: *She got sent home for her bra strap showing?*

Son: *Well, she also got her belly button pierced over the weekend, so she had to wear low-rise jeans so it wouldn't hurt and her thong showed in the back when she sat down and apparently that's a second violation. It's insane. They don't own our bodies.*

Mom: *Seems like they keep making stricter rules at your school. Why do you think they would do that?*

This back-and-forth can lead to a conversation—that may take place in fits and starts over weeks, months, or years—about how sexy ads intentionally reinforce the impression that very revealing dress is normal and suitable for kids (just like the super-casual hookups on television and in the movies). Parents can add that they understand that provocative clothes may help spice up the school day for students, but that modest dress can help both students and teachers focus on their work and protect them from distraction.

In conversations like these, your teen may vehemently disagree with your ideas or accuse you of being an old ninny. Consider these talks a kind of conversation with the unconscious. You've introduced your point of view. Trust that your observations, like medication that is released into the bloodstream over a period of time, will slowly be absorbed into your teenager's mind.

Talking about your sexual history
Although teenagers don't like to talk or think about your current sex life, they may be quite capable of asking nosy questions about your youthful escapades. Daughters tend to ask their mothers about their sexual history more often than boys ask their fathers. The girls ask in the spirit of, "I'm just trying to see what kind of woman I should be. I want to be like you."

However, you are under no obligation to provide full disclosure of your past. Maybe your daughter wants to know how old you were the first time you had sex. If she had asked when you last had sex, would you feel compelled to tell her? Of course you wouldn't, because it's private business. Parents sometimes feel that if they don't honestly answer every question about sex (or drugs) they are being inauthentic, but consider this another opportunity to practice good truthiness. Your past is your property and it is embedded in a deep personal and cultural context. When you set boundaries by keeping the selected details to yourself, you protect the sanctity of your personal history and protect your child from information he is not yet ready to understand.

But what if you *want* to talk about your history? Then take a page out of their playbook. Teens often test parent reactions by talking about a friend when they are actually talking about themselves:

I have this friend who is thinking about kissing another girl.

You can do the same:

I had a friend in junior high (that's what middle school was called then) who had sex at fourteen because . . .

> *she wanted to punish her parents for being so strict.*
> *she was pressured by her boyfriend and didn't know how to say no.*
> *she was a sad girl whose parents traveled all the time.*
> *her boyfriend was her comfort, they were like—have you ever heard this*
>   *phrase?—orphans in a storm.*

Supplement sex ed with books

Talk frequently about your sexual values, but when it comes to the mechanics of sex, lean on books to help you out. The depth of health science classes in most middle and high schools is uneven. Don't believe teens when they insist, "I learned all about sex in seventh grade! I know everything." They don't. Sexuality and safe sex practices are complicated, and a few lectures, even good ones, are not sufficiently comprehensive to cover all the questions that will emerge over time. Meanwhile, the legendary "talks" that fathers are supposed to have with their sons, and mothers with their daughters, often fall flat. Even the most liberated parents can balk at showing their thirteen-year-old son how to put a condom on a banana. The beauty of a book is that it can be read and reread as often as necessary. Earlier, I mentioned *Dr. Ruth's Guide to Teens and Sex Today: From Social Networking to Friends with Benefits.* Here are a few more of my favorites:

For younger teens I recommend the "What's Happening to My Body" book series with separate volumes for girls and boys. Both are written by the mother-and-daughter author team of Lynda and Area Madaras.

Changing Bodies, Changing Lives: A Book for Teens on Sex and Relationships, by Ruth Bell. This is encyclopedic, very frank, and better for older teens.

Everything You NEVER Wanted Your Kids to Know About Sex but Were Afraid They'd Ask, by Justin Richardson and Mark Schuster. Written by two medical doctors, this book for parents is a gem—wry, clear, and astute. The authors offer lots of scenarios, scripts, and stories to help support, guide, and educate parents about this delicate but critical subject matter. Sample chapter titles include: "But If You Do . . . The Art and Science of Encouraging Safer Sex" and "And So It Begins: Parenting Your Sexually Active Child, from the First Time On."

MISSION: DELIGHT

The hardest thing about teaching your children about enjoying earthly pleasures responsibly and with moderation is setting an example of delight yourself. In a discussion about the fallout from the locker-room video scandal I mentioned earlier, I asked the parents to think about their own sex lives. One mother raised her hand high in the air. She said, "Sex life? Are you kidding? We are sooooo tired. We cart the scholar-princes around all afternoon—from practices, to SAT prep, to band rehearsals. Then we come home and fall asleep catatonic by nine o'clock."

This is an entirely unintended consequence of parental devotion: We neglect to make adulthood attractive to our sons and daughters. To many teenagers, adulthood appears to be little more than an opportunity to resolve complex scheduling conflicts, get stuck in freeway traffic, curse at the computer, and fall asleep long, long before they do. In a recent high school survey, one student wrote, "I don't know what I want to be when I grow up, but I know what I don't want to be. I don't want to be like my mom and dad. They seem so sad and scared and stressed." Teens like these are at risk for a carpe diem approach to adolescence: "Seize the day, for tomorrow you shall be nervous grown-ups."

The rabbis recognized that it is easy to be seduced by work and worry—in modern times, this means fretting about paying tuition and making sure our kids make their flashcards so they'll pass the test so they'll get into college so they'll get a job in this unsettled world. This is why, in Judaism, delight is directly and consistently linked to holiness. Seeking pleasure and happiness in this world, not waiting for *olam haba,* the "world to come," is a central Jewish commandment. On his deathbed, the third-century rabbi Judah the Prince is said to have raised his hands and confessed to God, "It is known to you that I have not enjoyed the pleasures of this world even with my little finger." Why was he moved to confess? Because in *olam haba* God will take us to task for every legitimate pleasure we refused to enjoy. The rabbis teach that it is our acts in *olam hazeh* (this world) that matter and that it is arrogant and disrespectful to God to reject the glorious opportunities offered us. Seeking and finding sensual delight is a way to honor God, to say, *Thanks for all this stuff (my body, your bounty). I'm taking care to seek balance, to not abuse it or take it for granted. I'm making this a priority.*

As a parent, you have a heightened obligation to experience pleasure because, by watching you, your children will learn the value of delight and sensuality. As the parent of a teenager, you have a double challenge: to show your children that you can enjoy yourself even while doing an unusually difficult job—raising them. Sensual delights confer an additional benefit. They provide emotional fuel so that you will be refreshed and patient when your teenager tries your nerves.

Practice taking pleasure in whatever form you prefer: private jokes with your best friend, trading foot rubs with your mate, the perfect mojito, hiking on a warm day with a pack filled with a frozen water bottle and tangerines. Demonstrate a healthy attitude toward sex by implication. Show warmth toward your spouse or partner. Compliment him or her in front of the children. Tend to the decoration of your bedroom as generously as the more public spaces in the house. As often as possible, go to bed at the same time as your partner, and spend a decent amount of time there with the door closed and locked. This will be enough to signal that you and your spouse enjoy being alone together.

Remember that your teenager is listening, watching, studying intently, eager to learn. If your teens observe you enjoying yourself—if they understand that there are specific pleasures that attend adulthood—they will be comforted by your contentment. A friend told me this illuminating story: She and her husband were in the bedroom, door closed, not having sex but just relaxing and laughing together for a long time. Later her college freshman daughter, home for the summer, said, "You know, kids like to hear that sound. It makes them feel happy because they know their parents are happy."

CHAPTER 10

The Courage to Let Them Go

After Isaac blessed his son Jacob, he and Rebecca sent him off to find a wife. On the first day of his journey, young Jacob traveled until the sun set. Weary and ready for sleep, he took a stone, put it under his head, and bedded down under the stars. That night he had a vivid dream. In it a ladder was set on the ground, and, according to the passage in Genesis, "Its top reached the sky and behold! Angels of God were ascending and descending on it." Next, God appeared in Jacob's dream and said, "Remember, I am with you. I will protect you wherever you go." When Jacob first woke up, he was shaken by this vision of all these busy angels and of God speaking directly to him.

Rashi, the great medieval commentator on the Torah, explains that the angels in Jacob's dream were *sar,* protective angels who are unseen by those they escort. Rashi makes a distinction between the ascending angels who belonged to the Babylonian kingdom, and who had accompanied Jacob up to this point in his life, and the descending or "diaspora" angels. When Jacob reached the borders of his homeland, a ladder appeared because the ascending angels were being replaced with those who would protect him as he ventured outside of the land of Israel.

When teenagers head off to college or a gap year or another sort of post–high school adventure, they are usually bursting with happy anticipation. They may be worried, but the prospect of a release from parental oversight and intrusion is thrilling.

Shortly after the journey begins, however, they will begin to doubt their navigation skills. When darkness falls, they will find themselves weary and homesick. Like Jacob, they note that the bed offered to them is not the one they know and love. "Mom," they say when calling home, "I can't sleep here. We picked out the wrong pillow! It feels like a rock!"

For a few shaky weeks or months, your child may focus only on the absence of their old angels: parents and old friends and favorite teachers, the ones who protected them in their homeland. At first, they won't be able to recognize those who might help them in this new unfamiliar territory. But the resilient adolescent sojourner, the one who has been allowed to experience the consequences of breaking rules, losing sweaters, and writing B minus papers, is prepared for these challenges. Given time to acclimate to the new environment, and encouraged by an unalarmed, kind, and confident voice from a seasoned parent at home, they will find that new angels await them on every rung: resident advisers who live in the dorm, deans, peer tutors, counselors, coworkers, apartment roommates, employers, and professor angels who materialize in the lecture hall and during special angel office hours. Your child may find an angel in a new friend's parents, the ones who invite her to visit their homes during vacation, the ones who make lasagna or blueberry pie and invite some nice neighbors for dinner, too. I know a young man who found an angel on a bus. Spencer had grown up and ably made his way around two big cities, New York and Philadelphia, but when he attended the University of Pittsburgh, he kept getting lost. When he confessed this persistent problem to a bus driver who had just prevented him from getting off at the wrong stop, the driver explained: "You have to forget the grid you're used to. In this city we use our hundred bridges and hills and rivers as landmarks. Then you stay oriented. You always know where you are."

If you want your child to recognize these new angels descending from ladders all around, you must ascend your own ladder. Don't hover too long on the first or second rung, calling to wake your child up for class, offering to edit papers, cross-examining him about what he ate for dinner, or even attempting too effortfully to mend a broken heart. Climbing the ladder is a test of *bitachon,* of faith in your child's resourcefulness and the goodwill of others, of faith in new mentors, bus drivers, and the sturdiness of bridges and hills and rivers. Take comfort in the insight Jacob gained once he'd had a chance to reflect on his strange dream. Recognizing its majesty, he reevaluated his situation. "How awesome it is here," he thought. "Surely God is in this place and I, I did not know." Sensing a protective presence, he confidently resumed his journey.

Have enough faith to let go, but allow yourself to feel heartbroken that your child is gone. One father, a corporate executive, warned his daughter that when he said good-bye to her in her college dorm room he expected it to be the saddest day of his life. It was. To him and to you I offer an excerpt from a poem by Lydia Davis about the power of talking respectfully to yourself about missing a loved one. It's called "Head, Heart":

> *Heart weeps.*
> *Head tries to help heart.*
> *Head tells heart how it is, again:*
> *You will lose the ones you love. . . .*
> *Heart feels better, then.*
> *But the words of head do not remain long in the ears of heart.*
> *Heart is new to this.*
> *I want them back, says heart.*
> *Head is all heart has.*
> *Help, head. Help heart.*

Your grief is right and proper. It is a measure of your love and devotion. Parental heartbreak often hides or disguises itself in worries and fretfulness. Prepare yourself for this, too. You are in unfamiliar emotional territory now and you also need new angels. After building the habits of prodding and ushering and supporting and tending, it can be hard to pull back and simply look up and around and forward. But you will.

And then, one day, after your child has been on his perilous and interesting and fulfilling journey for a good long time, he'll return to visit his homeland. He'll smile at the old "Keep Out" sign, if you've left it on his door, and say his grown-up version of the words you miss from his childhood: "Lie down with me. Don't go." But this time it will be mutual. "Are you going to bed now? It's so good to be here, sitting in the kitchen. Can we stay up and talk a while longer? Can I make you a cup of tea? How are *you* doing?"

Acknowledgments

I am indebted to Leigh Ann Hirschman, an editor of unusual grace, equanimity, and ready laughter. Thank you, Leigh Ann, for being such a devoted and bold architect, surgeon, and choreographer. Samantha Martin, my editor at Scribner, I am grateful for your endurance, good sense, and compassionate understanding of the difficulty of letting go. Thank you to the droll and worldly Betsy Amster, my literary agent for a decade, and to my lecture agent, Debbie Greene, whose charm, persistence, and deft hand allow my ideas about parenting to make their way smoothly around the country over and over again.

To all the mental health, school counselor, school administrator, and student advocate colleagues: Reveta Bowers, Michael Brosnan, Sharon Merrow Cuseo, the late Carol Eliot, Dr. Gary Emery, Mary Fauvre, Terry Kung, Patty Lancaster, Dr. Marcia Leikin, Dr. Sheila Siegal, Fran Scoble, and to Dr. Madeline Levine and Dr. Denise Clark Pope of the "Challenge Success" project at Stanford for their conviction that protecting adolescents from damaging levels of stress can be taken to the level of public policy and who believe, as the feminists did when they cried "Take back the night," that we can take back the children.

Thank you also to the parents of the Harvard-Westlake and Crossroads School for submitting fifty-two pointed and heartfelt questions and to Barbara Deutsch, a middle school teacher at the Joseph Kushner Hebrew Academy in Livingston, New Jersey, who said, "It's helpful to think of teenagers as pregnant. They're changing every day. They are preparing to give birth to themselves." And to the woman who, after a lecture many years ago, handed me a little cloth bag filled with Jewish blessings printed on small pieces of paper: Thank you for introducing me to the blessing used in the epigraph of this book.

To friends and family: my candid and exuberant niece, Theadora Tolkin, for her reflections on college life; to Laurie Goodman—dear friend!—thanks for anecdotes from the trenches and comfort and perspective when I found myself sinking into either parenting or writing troughs of gloom; to folklorist Jane Beck for welcoming me into a tribe that congratulates children for jumping into the lake from an impossibly tall boathouse roof; to Darcy Vebber, who can fish in ancient Jewish texts and pull out elegant solutions to modern problems; to Patricia Moss-Vreeland, fine artist and fine friend since fifth grade and the "Patty" of the summer-camp hitchhiking story; and to the teenagers of my neighborhood who amaze me by always inquiring with genuine interest, "And how are you, Wendy?"—Jess, Abby, Mere, Olivia K., Olivia L., and Taylor.

Thanks to my ever-ready assistant, Kara Wall, who always gets it. And then takes care of it, too.

And especially to my daughters, Susanna and Emma, who inspire me by their diverse passions and fierce devotion to following their own path, and to my husband, Michael Tolkin, who, for the forty years since we first started a long conversation, has helped me understand precisely how everything fits together.

Index

goals, executive functions in setting of, 53

God, 7, 47
  adolescents in image of, 11, 123
  in the details, 50–51
  discomfort with term, 40
  as protective but detached, 96
  trust in, 16, 40, 102
  and use of alcohol, 157–58
Goleman, Daniel, 24
good deprivation, 91–93
good longing, 91
good suffering, 97–103
grades, 25
  low, 4, 54–55
gratitude, prayers of, 4
"green beret" mentality, 115
grief of separation, 2, 16–17, 179

"handicapped royalty," 50, 53, 56
havadalah, 120
"Head, Heart" (Davis), 179
help-rejecting complainers, 16
hiddur mitzvah, 157
Hillel, Rabbi, 30
homework, 49–69
  deflating drama of, 52–57
  distractions to, 56
  in sleep loss, 129–30
  vs. chores and work, 57, 66–67
Honi the Circle Maker, 152–53
hookups vs. commitment, 169, 170–72
How Do I Decide? (Gittlesohn), 169
humor, adolescent, 17, 126–27
Hungry Clothes and Other Jewish Folktales, The (Schram), 152
hypocrisy, 151–52

idealism, 81
  and moodiness, 27
  and self-centeredness, 141
identified patient (IP), 138

identity, forming of, 4, 60
"idiot compassion," 113
immaturity, 21–23, 26, 136
individuality:
  acceptance of, 9–12
  clothing and personal appearance as expressive of, 27
  uniqueness and, 9–28, 145
inebriation, 159
  see also alcohol use and abuse
insecurity, as escalated by media, 107–10, 125, 169, 170
inspiration, in learning curve, 53
insults, insulting behavior, 36–37
  see also rudeness
integrity, *see* ethics, ethical behavior
Internet, 52, 108, 129–30, 170
  maturity guidelines for use of, 125–26
  overcoming fear of, 124–26
  sexual websites on, 169
internships, 63–64
Isaac, 47, 177
"I" statements, 34–35
Ivy League schools, 24, 145

Jews, Judaism, 5, 7, 14, 17, 24, 28, 41, 47
  actions vs. beliefs in, 30, 51, 52
  basic, 3
  as connection to history and community, 117, 158
  Exodus as adolescence of, 3–4
  moderation in, 156–59
  pleasure and happiness as holy in, 174–76
  preserving spirit of, 118
  respect in, 30–31
  rituals of, 3, 26; *see also individual holidays*
  use of alcohol in, 157–59
Judah the Prince, 175
junk pleasures, 127–28

About the Author

Wendy Mogel, Ph.D., is a clinical psychologist, parent educator, keynote speaker for educational and religious organizations and schools, and the author of the *New York Times* bestseller *The Blessing of a Skinned Knee*. She lives in Los Angeles. Please visit her website at www.wendymogel.com.